Y0-AAJ-986

BIBLIOGRAPHY: *Tiger or Fat Cat?*

BIBLIOGRAPHY

Tiger or Fat Cat?

by

PAUL S. DUNKIN

ARCHON BOOKS
1975

Library of Congress Cataloging in Publication Data

Dunkin, Paul Shaner, 1905-
    Bibliography, tiger or fat cat?

    Includes index.
    1. Bibliography.   I. Title.
Z1001.D83   010   75-5634
ISBN 0-208-01519-1

Z
1001
.D83

© 1975 by The Shoe String Press, Inc.,
First published 1975 as an Archon Book,
an imprint of The Shoe String Press, Inc.,
Hamden, Connecticut 06514

All rights reserved

Printed in the United States of America

Library
UNIVERSITY OF MIAMI

Contents

Prologue

A Bow and a Step,

Then a Question and a List

This is a book about Bibliography. It is the custom to open such a discourse with the remark that "Bibliography" once meant writing books and that only in the nineteenth century did the word come to mean writing about books. It is the custom then to define Bibliography more closely, to tell what we may write about books. Finally it is the custom for the writer to seize upon that activity of Bibliography to which he is addicted and call it simply "Bibliography" and discuss it as elaborately as what he thinks he knows and the space at his disposal will allow.

To this custom I bow, and at once I step into the prescribed definition.

Any definition of Bibliography is a statement of personal experience and belief. In 1950 Percy Freer listed fifty definitions since 1678, most of them since 1900 (*Bibliography and Modern Book Production*, 1-13). Few of these definitions agree completely; many differ widely. Even statements at different times by the same author do not always agree. Probably this is true also of statements since 1950. The following definition is, therefore, not final. It is offered simply as a framework on which to hang a discussion.

Bibliography has one main purpose: To locate books. It may

locate one book (e.g., in a descriptive article in a journal); or it may locate several, or even many, books (e.g., in a finding list). Bibliography locates books by one or more of at least three kinds of analysis:

1. *Physical Analysis.* The study of books as physical objects is called Analytical Bibliography, and it locates each book in relation to other editions, issues, and copies of that book. The product may be called Descriptive Bibliography or Descriptive Cataloging, the arrangement of books or lists of books in terms of their physical characteristics. Analytical Bibliography may also help in Textual Criticism, an activity we shall examine much later in some detail.

2. *Subject Analysis.* This locates each book in relation to other books on the same or other subjects. The product is the arrangement of books or lists of books by such devices as subject headings or subject classification.

3. *Author and/or Title Analysis.* This locates each book in relation to other books with the same or other authors and/or titles. The product is author and/or title arrangement of books or lists of books.

The list resulting from any of these three kinds of analysis may be called an Enumerative Bibliography.

This book will examine only Analytical Bibliography. And here again I bow to the custom set forth above: From now on I shall call Analytical Bibliography simply Bibliography.

Bibliography, I have suggested, looks at the book as a physical object. It is not primarily the study of the pretty book. The pretty book is all very well for those who like it; indeed, Bibliography may have begun with the study of the pretty book by or for book collectors. But basically the book is not often (and then only incidentally) a work of art; instead it is simply a means of communication. The physical form of the book determines how well it communicates—cf. the effect of the papyrus roll and the paper codex or handwriting and printing on ease of reading. In the present work Bibliography looks at the physical book as a printed paper codex.

Probably there is general agreement about two features of Bibliography:

1. Ronald B. McKerrow's *An Introduction to Bibliography for Literary Students* (1927) was and remains a landmark statement of the study and its aims. (Quotations from McKerrow are by permission of Oxford University Press, Oxford, England.)
2. In the half century since McKerrow's book, Bibliography has taken giant strides in many directions, frequently directions foreshadowed by McKerrow. The leaders in the march have been Sir Walter Greg and Professor Fredson Bowers.

We now face a basic question. Bowers has compared the growth of Bibliography with the growth of a tabby cat into a tiger (BSA *Papers* 46[1952]189). In real life cats may grow into fat cats but they seem never to grow into tigers.

Has Bibliography become a tiger or has it become a fat cat?

In the following pages I suggest some answers to this question. I do not try to give a full account of Bibliography. Instead, I offer only a few comments on a casual survey of what some bibliographers have done and said in some sections of their domain. I do not write only for bibliographers. I write also for the users of Bibliography, and I try to write in the language of everyday. No doubt my remarks now and again reflect my ignorance and my prejudice.

And now a list. References to books and articles appear within parentheses alongside the appropriate statements. Many are complete enough to stand alone. But reference to each of the following studies is only by the author's surname or by the indicated abbreviation. (In no sense is this list a bibliography of bibliography.)

Bowers, Fredson. *Principles of Bibliographical Description* (1949).
Foxon, David F. *Thoughts on the History and Future of Bibliographical Description* (1970).
Gaskell, Philip. *A New Introduction to Bibliography* (1972).
Hinman, Charlton. *The Printing and Proof-Reading of the First Folio of Shakespeare* (1963).
Greg, Sir Walter. *A Bibliography of the English Printed Drama to the Restoration* (1939-59).

Jackson, William A. *Bibliography & Literary Studies* (1962).

McKenzie, D. F. "Printers of the Mind: Some Notes on Bibliographical Theories and Printing-House Practices" in *Studies in Bibliography* 22(1969)1-75.

McKerrow, Ronald B. *An Introduction to Bibliography for Literary Students* (1927).

Moxon, Joseph. *Mechanick Exercises on the Whole Art of Printing (1683-4)* ed. by Herbert Davis & Harry Carter (2d ed., 1962).

The Papers of the Bibliographical Society of America. Cited as BSA *Papers.*

Savage, William. *A Dictionary of the Art of Printing* (1841).

Standards of Bibliographical Description, by Curt F. Bühler, James G. McManaway, Lawrence C. Wroth (1949). Cited as *Standards.*

Stokes, Roy. *The Function of Bibliography* (1969).

Studies in Bibliography, Papers of the Bibliographical Society of the University of Virginia. Cited as *SB.*

The Bibliographical Society, 1892-1942, Studies in Retrospect (1945). Cited as *Stud. in Retro.*

Thorpe, James. *Principles of Textual Criticism* (1972).

Part One

Whose Cause I Serve
His Tongue I Speak.

Bibliography, I have suggested, is the study of books as physical objects. Like every study, Bibliography can be useful only if the bibliographer tells other people what his study has taught him. Without the telling, Bibliography is the flower born to blush unseen and waste its sweetness on the desert air.

Tells what other people? The answer decides the language of the telling.

From the first, Bibliography claimed the rank of a handmaiden science. McKerrow wrote his famous *Introduction* not for would-be bibliographers writing for Bibliography's sake, but for "literary students" because Bibliography would help them in their study of the "transmission of texts". Others have agreed: Curt F. Buhler: "Bibliography is not so much an end in itself as it is an ancillary investigation to the study of the text (be it literary, historical, or scientific)" (*Standards* 8). Lawrence C. Wroth: "Bibliography is not an end but a means, a process in the study of the transmission of texts" (*Standards* 105). Bowers was somewhat more restrictive: "True bibliography is the bridge to textual, which is to say literary, criticism" (9).

Actually, of course, many books studied and described by

bibliographers will never be issued in modern editions with elaborate apparatus criticus. The precise texts of most Latin theology, science and literary works printed as incunabula have little significance today. At the other extreme, who expects scholarly editions of this year's best sellers—or even learned notes on a crucial phrase? A bibliography of a printer might well include several books which no one ever intends to read or refer to in any edition. The exact wording of a Puritan tract or a Reformation pamphlet may never be needed by anyone. The list could go on forever.

No one will deny that it is worthwhile for bibliographers to study such books and tell of what they find. "For in the ultimate resort," wrote Greg, "the object of bibliographical study is, I believe, to reconstruct for each particular book the history of its life, to make it reveal in its most intimate detail the story of its birth and adventures as a material vehicle of the living word. As an extension of this follows the investigation of the methods of production in general and of the conditions of survival" (*Stud. in Retro.* 27).

All this is meat and drink for Bowers' textual critic, the scholar who seeks an author's precise original words and phrases. But it is also on the diet of the historian of literature, the historian of printing and publishing, the historian of science, the historian of economics, the historian of religion, the historian of almost anything. "Bibliography, in my opinion, is an ancillary science. . . . The study of the physical book . . . has uses that no student of history or of the historical aspects of any other subject can safely neglect." Edwin E. Willoughby then went on to prove his statement by describing "a number of problems which might have resisted other methods of solution" than the methods of bibliography (*Uses of Bibliography* (1957) 17-18). Finally, there is the librarian who uses bibliography to help him seek books for all scholars. Bibliography, it seems, is handmaiden to many.

At the other extreme Bowers drew a drastic conclusion from the relation of Bibliography and Textual Criticism: "I should like to view analytical bibliography as by definition a pure method, and critical bibliography as its application to immediate and specific problems. . . . It must follow that analytical bibliography should be allowed to pursue its own investigations in its own way without being forced to justify itself, at least as a principle, by the necessity for practical application in the service of humane studies. . . . Analytical bibliography . . . by its nature is truly written for other 'bibliographers and not for literary students" (BSA *Papers* 46[1952]198-200). "Bibliography in its several essential forms is, I hold, an end in itself and not a means to an end; it is an independent discipline of scholarship and not merely an ancillary technique to literary investigation" (*Library* 5th ser. 8[1953]22). Geoffrey Keynes suggested that "this tendency to exaggerate the claims of bibliography until it comes to be an end rather than a means is perhaps to be recognized as a psychological frustration. If the ego cannot get satisfaction by creating something for itself, let it at least gain reflected glory by hanging on to the coat-tails of the true artists, until it may seem in its own eyes after all to have created something shining with the lustre of pure scholarship." He had sympathy for "academic bibliographers" because "Finding themselves in the company of scholars, who need to be convinced that bibliography really has serious claims on their attention, they instinctively react by behaving as a small persecuted minority. They are forced to push their technical specialty in order to be taken seriously" (*Library* 5th ser. 8[1953]66).

In any event, there are at least four different notions about the other people for whom the bibliographer writes: (1) They are textual critics; or (2) They are students in many areas, chiefly historical; or (3) They are librarians; or (4) They are other bibliographers. The first three notions suggest that the bibliographer tell what he has found in every day language; the fourth allows a jargon of bibliographers to grow up.

A bibliographer tells one or more of at least three things about a book he has examined as a physical object: (1) He classifies it as an edition, issue, state, or variant; (2) He transcribes its title; (3) He states its collation. We shall look at each of these jobs in some detail.

1. *What Is This and What Is That?*

We begin with McKerrow: "No precise definition of 'issue' or 'edition' is possible, but there is among bibliographers a well-recognized difference in the use of the two words. In modern times we can define 'edition' as the whole number of copies of a book printed at any time or times from one setting-up of type. . . . By 'issue' is generally meant some special form of the book in which, for the most part, the original sheets are used but which differs from the earlier or normal form by the addition of new material or by some difference in arrangement. . . . The word is, however, very loosely used . . ."(175).

McKerrow's approach was lucid and relaxed. Most importantly, it recognized the conventional view that classification as edition and issue need be based only on easily recognized physical differences between the variant forms in which the book may appear and that strict uniformity in use of the term does not greatly matter. The attitude of McKerrow's first paragraph dominated the following pages in which he discussed classifications possible with a number of specific difficult problems.

Bowers, however, felt that the history of the printing of a particular variant, rather than its physical characteristics alone, should decide its classification (37-123 and BSA *Papers* 41[1947] 271-292). He introduced two new terms: "An *ideal copy* is that form of the book which the printer or publisher wished to represent the most perfect and complete form to leave his shop . . . alterations or additions made to constitute *ideal copy* may be called *states*, whether made before or after publication; and only alterations or additions important enough to cause a cancellans title to be printed to call attention to them constitute *re-issue*" (BSA *Papers* 41[1947]290). Also he urged that strict uniformity of classification is necessary for reference purposes and as a help to further study of the variant.

On the whole Greg agreed with much of the Bowers approach; although his "Provisional Memoranda" (vol. 1) did not mention classification, his discussion of classification (vol. 4, xxxii-xlii) was less rigid than Bowers; and he used the term "variant" instead of "state." Also his list of corrections in vol. 4 did not include a number of classifications in vol. 1 which had not conformed to the Bowers distinctions—e.g., vol. 1, p. 162, 210, 243, 273, 290, 345, 381, 391, 449.

With the Bowers-Greg approach, only a bibliographer can say that a book belongs to an issue or state because only he has the technical knowledge and the time needed to reconstruct its printing and publishing history. This means that most books will never be classified at all because most books never receive a bibliographer's attention. Moreover, the terminology will not help solve bibliographical problems (as Bowers urged it would) because all problems must be solved before the terminology can be applied. Bibliographers will not have a language in which they can talk with one another about newly discovered or unexplained variants.

Probably Bibliography needs more universal terms if it is to serve widely. Ideally, they would be terms understood at once by scholars, not merely by bibliographers. On the other hand, they would be terms any student could apply himself without benefit of bibliographer. The moment he came across a copy of a book which differed from another copy he should have a name for it. The new terminology is not universal in this sense.

The plain fact, of course, is that an infinitely greater number of books are listed in catalogs than are described in bibliographies. As a result, there is much more cross-reference between catalogs and catalogs or between catalogs and bibliographies than between bibliographies and other bibliographies. If uniformity for reference purposes is necessary, it will be useful and, indeed, possible only if it depends on the definitions currently used by catalogers as well as by bibliographers—i.e., distinctions based on easily recognized physical differences between variants. More of this later.

It is true that Bowers has stated specifically again and again that he is concerned only with Bibliography which leads to Textual Criticism. At the same time, Bowers' extensive remarks about incunabula and modern books, and his suggestion that a descriptive bibliography could be compiled for a non-literary group of books such as the output of a printer, seem to indicate that he may have had in mind also the broader fields of bibliographical study in which textual criticism has slight importance.

Many writers on book collecting have lamented the lack of precise and uniform definitions and then tried to construct them in terms of publishing history; cf. the remarks under "Issues and States" in the various editions of John Carter's *ABC for Book Collectors*. This is only natural for, after all, the fun in collecting comes with owning a "first" and how can you know what is the first state of the first issue unless you talk in terms of publishing? The new terminology seeks to merge the two ideas, to graft the collector's specific buying term onto the scholar's loose reference term and create a specific reference term.

This union of publishing history and physical differences ignores the fact that publishers do not always think like bibliographers. McKerrow once remarked that although the bibliographer thinks of the book as a material object, "the purchaser as a rule buys a book with the intention of reading it. . . . The publisher's business is to sell books to readers" and therefore "he would be wise to accept the reader's point of view. . . . It seems advisable for a publisher to talk of a 'new edition' when and only when (1) the literary content is altered; (2) the form is altered by a change in size, type, quality of paper, binding, etc. . . . A mere re-setting of a book word for word in the same type would not be called a new edition (it is, of course, a new impression, as any reprint is), while a re-issue of the original sheets, cut down and in a cheaper binding would be so called. . . . Edition would thus be used quite differently in a bibliography (whether of old or modern books) and in a publisher's catalogue; but I cannot see that any confusion would result" (*TLS* [1931]760).

The Bowers definitions insist on publishing history. But they are not concerned with publisher's intention to create what the publisher himself considered an edition, issue, or state. Rather it is publishing history which resulted in physical changes recognized by Bowers as creating edition, issue, or state.

The Bowers effort to get an exact definition for every possible variant was thorough (37-123 and 371-426). First came an elaborate statement of broad general definitions; then some 100 pages packed with detailed discussion, intricate distinctions, and illuminating illustrations. Any one of five conditions might result in a variant state; any one of three, a re-issue; any one of another three, a separate issue; and any one of four, an edition.

Many of these fifteen conditions were subdivided; the first, for instance, had five sub-classes. Also involved were rather extensive modifications Bowers wanted for modern books. There appear to be a few inconsistencies in the scheme. With early books, for instance, both physical make-up and printer's and publisher's intention are needed to create an "issue" while for the far more important group called an "edition" only one aspect of physical make-up, the setting of type, is required (39-40 and elsewhere). For early books a "re-issue" must almost always have a cancel title page while for modern books the cancel is often not necessary (41 and 403-4). In modern books "editions" result not only from a different setting of type but also from publisher's intention so that what in early books would be "issues" or even "states" are in modern books sometimes "sub-editions" (388, 393, 395, 419 especially), and so on.

Finally, classification based on history of the printing and publication of a book rests on shifting sand. "What escapes one generation as bibliographical evidence may be found crucial in the next" (Bowers, 138, n. 6). It can happen even when a first-rate bibliographer does the classifying. Greg, for instance, described the 1609 *Troilus and Cressida* as existing in two issues, one differing from the other in that two conjugate leaves bearing a new title and an address to the reader cancelled the original title page (No. 279). Philip Williams, Jr., however, then showed that the cancel leaves were probably printed, as a part of continuous printing, with the final two-leaf gathering of the book (*SB* 2[1949]25-33). "It follows that there are not two issues . . . but merely two states" (Greg vol. 4, 1679) because the cancellation was made only to constitute ideal copy before publication. Even Curt F. Bühler and Bowers once had problems with an "ideal copy" (*SB* 15[1962]219-222).

Bibliography, we must remember, is an historical study and like all historical studies must perforce deal with inexact terms. Who, for instance can define "Middle Class" or "Renaissance" or "Puritan" to the complete satisfaction of his neighbor? We must redefine a term every time we use it. Perhaps this is true also of "state" and "issue."

We cannot (using Greg's original classification) say simply "the issue of *Troilus and Cressida*" or (using Bowers' classification) say simply "the state," because there are, after all, two of them whether we call them "issues" or "states." We must say "the cancel issue" or "the cancel state"; and "the issue without a cancel" or "the state without a cancel." The distinguishing feature, for reference purposes at least, is the physical characteristic, not the term applied to the group of variant copies which it produced.

So the new classification is jargon, but it is harmless.

2. *Title-Pages &c*

Again we begin with McKerrow: In transcribing the title a bibliographer "should take care never to elaborate his work beyond need, for if he does he will almost certainly . . . land himself in difficulties; and he should remember that a transcript of a title, however full and careful, is but a compromise. He cannot, whatever he does, give *all* the information . . . nor can he forsee exactly what information may be needed by a worker who consults his book." Transcription "may be of many degrees of elaboration, but . . . it will suffice to give two examples, one as full as is generally wanted, the other abbreviated, but so far as it goes correct" (147).

The "full" transcription gives such things as complete content, kinds (italic, black letter, roman) but not sizes of type, line endings, ornaments, and ligatures, with attention to the problems of I and J, V and U. The "abbreviated" transcription does not indicate line endings or kinds of type or full content, although it does mark omissions with the traditional three dots. Whichever form is used may be applied also to transcription of the colophon.

As in his approach to classification, McKerrow was lucid, relaxed, and conventional.

Greg began his *Bibliography* with the simple statement that "transcripts of title-pages &c. follow, in the main, standard methods (as laid down, for example . . . by R. B. McKerrow . . .)," accompanied by a page of examples (vol. 1, xv-xvi). In the end, when he wrote his "Excursus III" on transcription (vol. 4, cxxxi-cxlviii), he began: "The method . . . aims at reproducing the original as exactly as can with convenience be done in the course of a continuous paragraph." He then stated in some detail what he had done, with no suggestion that this should be standardized practice, although his monumental bibliography is its own argument for standardization.

With Bowers (135-192) we moved into a more rigid world. "The chief bibliographical purpose . . . is to provide all practicable information necessary for a minute comparison of any individual copy with the published transcript in order to confirm its precise identity or to establish variation" (135). The notion that simplified transcription is "sufficiently accurate to detect differences in title-pages" is a "naive assertion . . . simply not borne out by the facts. Quasi-facsimile remains the only accurate method of transcription yet devised by which a title-page can be compared for variation in setting with reasonable prospect of success" (138-139). "What escapes one generation as bibliographical evidence may be found crucial in the next. Of more importance . . . a bibliographer may not be aware" of all variant copies of his book (138, n.6). There was only one problem: lack of standardization. "Certain symbols are used by various writers to mean completely different things"; and "there is no uniformity among writers as to the degree of minuteness esteemed practicable"—e.g., treatment of swash italic capitals (139). Then came some fifty pages of rules and examples to achieve standardization. Photographic reproductions, "although useful additions to transcription, are in fact inadequate substitutes" because the copy chosen for reproduction may have poor inking, paper imperfections, and "various accretions" which "may reproduce as if they were punctuation" (136). Now and again he has returned to the fray with vigor—e.g., *Library* 5th ser. 8(1953)1-22 and 5th ser. 24(1969)89-128.

Ironically McKerrow's warning that the bibliographer should never transcribe too elaborately because, no matter what he does, he cannot "forsee exactly what information may be needed" thus became Bowers' warning that the bibliographer should use quasi-facsimile because "What escapes one generation as bibliographical evidence may be found crucial in the next."

There appears to be some evidence that elaborate transcription may not generally be necessary to separate editions, issues, and states, known and unknown.

In 1946 Elizabeth Pierce reported on a careful comparison of elaborate and simplified transcriptions of titles for 2,504 books representing 198 titles: "No entry failed to be identified through the simplified cataloging when it would have been identified through full transcription." Indeed, "the element indicating reliably an edition or issue is not on the title-page but in the collation: the main paging" (Library of Congress, *Studies of Descriptive Cataloging* [1946] 36-39).

Foxon suggested that quasi-facsimile transcription seems to have been devised independently by two men: Edward Capell in the eighteenth century and Falconer Madan in the late nineteenth century, each wanting only to "help the reader visualize the title—an antiquarian interest for Capell, a desire to show changes in layout in historical perspective for Madan" (18). The idea that elaborate transcription helps distinguish editions and issues Foxon considered only a rationalization of an already existing practice (17). With a study of Greg's *Bibliography* he found that "in almost every case a straightforward transcription of the title in roman type (without line endings) and the collation suffices to distinguish editions; only in three cases out of about a thousand is quasi-facsimile transcription necessary to distinguish editions, and in three further cases it fails to do the job" (19). Instead of troublesome and expensive quasi-facsimile, Foxon suggested Falconer Madan's "system of using signature positions to distinguish editions, possibly adopting Professor Todd's device of quoting the word under which the signature falls and italicizing the letters of that word which are directly over the signature" (20). (For signatures, collation, and gathering see p. 22-23.

Francis F. Madan's bibliography of the *Eikon Basilike* describes eighty-one editions of the work dated 1648-1904; a number of these editions consist of two or more issues each. Of these editions and issues only twenty have the same collation and paging as that of the entry immediately preceding—i.e., probably almost all but twenty can be individually identified by collation and pagination without regard to title transcription. Of these twenty entries for editions and issues, seven would differ from their preceding entries if they had brief title transcriptions, four would require quasi-facsimile, and nine would require descriptive notes regardless of how the title were transcribed— e.g., Madan's "no. 1, third issue" differs from "no. 1, second issue" in that the pagination of gathering G is corrected.

These three studies of transcription in the Library of Congress, in Greg's *Bibliography*, and in Madan's *Eikon Basilike* seem to suggest that:

1. Although quasi-facsimile transcription might help identify hitherto unknown editions and issues more fully, the number of known editions and issues identified by full title only is quite small—small enough to justify the calculated risk of briefer and simpler transcriptions.
2. Collation by gatherings and pagination are much more important than transcription in identifying editions and issues.
3. Some editions and issues cannot be identified even by quasi-facsimile transcription and collation by gatherings and pagination; in addition they require descriptive notes to set them apart.

Actually, of course, photographic reproduction makes academic all discussion of quasi-facsimile transcription. It is true that choice of a faulty title-page for photographic reproduction will result in misleading the reader as Bowers has warned (see above 19). But the time required for the bibliographer to choose a good copy (or to write a note warning if he has to use a bad copy) will surely be much less than the time required for quasi-facsimile transcription. Moreover, photographic reproduction will, even better than quasi-facsimile transcription, help the reader identify hitherto unnoted editions, issues, and states—to the limited extent that it is possible to identify them by titles alone.

Quasi-facsimile transcription began in the days before Xerox and microfilm when the bibliographer, traveling sometimes great distances to examine copies, needed a standard, detailed transcription against which he could match all copies. Then when he came to publish his bibliography he simply dumped his full transcription into the entry in his book for one or more of at least three reasons: (1) It was the custom, or (2) It was easier than to pick out what could be omitted, or (3) Just as quasi-facsimile transcription had helped him to find other copies, editions, issues, and states, so he hoped it might help his readers find still more copies, editions, issues, and states. He did not stop to measure these reasons against the cost of his work. It is sad to think of men of genius like Greg and Bowers pouring their time and energy into the clerical drudgery of copying out and proof reading long titles in barbaric type.

3. *ABC and * and Such*

For centuries the book as a physical object has been much the same. The basic unit is a gathering of leaves produced by folding a part of a large sheet, an entire large sheet, or several large sheets. A book may consist of one or more gatherings. Normally each gathering consists of an even number of leaves. The top side of a leaf is called its "recto"; the other side is the "verso." The recto of a leaf is a page, the verso is another page; each leaf, then, has two pages. The side of the large printed sheet which contains the first leaf recto (i.e., the first page) of that large sheet is called the "outer form" of the sheet; the side which contains the first leaf verso (i.e., the second page) is the "inner form."

Arrangement of the gatherings within the book is determined by "signatures." Signatures are printed in the bottom margins of the rectos of leaves. Generally, no more than the leaves in the first half of the gathering (but sometimes more or fewer leaves) are signed. This is particularly true of books printed before 1800; in more recent times it has become customary to sign only the first leaf of each gathering. There is a great variety in signatures. They may be letters; in that case the gatherings follow the sequence of the alphabet. They may be numerals with gatherings following a numerical sequence. They may be symbols with a normal or an arbitrary sequence—e.g., two gatherings signed * and ** would have an obvious sequence but gatherings signed * and & would have only an arbitrary sequence. In many modern books each gathering is marked on the edge of the outside fold in such a way that when the gatherings are arranged in proper sequence, the marks (called "back marks") will form a diagonal line across the spine of the book. This row of back marks is concealed when the book is bound. Gatherings of many incunabula are not signed in any way, and occasional unsigned gatherings occur in books of all periods.

The statement of the number of gatherings in a book and the number of leaves in each gathering we call the "collation" of the book. Collation not only makes clear the size and sequence of individual gatherings; collation also makes it possible to refer to individual leaves or pages or groups of leaves or pages. A collation may be judged by the ease with which the reader can understand its statement and use its system of reference.

Along with the statement of collation is a statement of format —i.e., the size and shape of the book in terms of how many leaves the folding of each large sheet has produced. Thus, a folio sheet has produced two leaves (four pages); a quarto, four leaves (eight pages); an octavo, eight leaves (16 pages); a duodecimo, twelve leaves (24 pages), and so on.

Also along with the statement of collation may be a statement of pagination or foliation; but collation by gatherings is much more useful because a book is an orderly group of gatherings, not a mere collection of pages or leaves. Many incorrect page or leaf numbers occur in early books but seldom any really misleading signatures; and often first or last leaves or pages of gatherings at the beginning or the end of the book are not numbered, although they are obviously part of the book as a physical object.

Below is an outline of McKerrow's suggested statement of collation and system of reference (155-163):

Statement (McKerrow)

Collation of "all but quite modern books is usually given in some such form as the following:

$*^2$, $**^6$, A-Z^6, Aa-Bb^6, Cc^4."

He then explains that this statement means that the book consists of the following segments:

> $*^2$ A two-leaf gathering in which the first leaf is unsigned if it is the title leaf and the second is signed $*^2$.
>
> $**^6$ A six-leaf gathering in which probably the first three or four leaves are signed $**$, $**2$, $**3$, $**4$.
>
> A-Z^6 Twenty-three six-leaf gatherings, signed with letters of the alphabet excluding J, U, and W.
>
> Aa-Bb^6 Two six-leaf gatherings signed Aa and Bb respectively.
>
> Cc^4 A four-leaf gathering signed Cc.

Thus, the whole book consists of: $2 + 6 + (23 \times 6) + (2 \times 6) + 4 = 162$ leaves.

Several special features of McKerrow's statement of collation are summarized below. (The numbering is my own.)

1. The number of leaves in a gathering is shown by the superior figure—e.g. A-Z^6.

2. If the series of alphabetical signatures is uninterrupted (except for the omission of J, U, and W) and the number of leaves in each gathering is the same it is necessary to record only the first letter and the last—e.g. A-Z^6. Irregularity, however, must be noted—e.g. B-C^6, E-M^6 if the printer produced no gathering A and no gathering D. A-W-Z if the printer used W as a signature. A-D^6, E^4, F-Z^6 if the printer used only four leaves in gathering E.

3. If the first gathering is unsigned, this may be recorded with brackets—e.g. []^2, A-Z^6.

But McKerrow thinks it would be "more convenient and much less unsightly" to use a "purely conventional 'signature' which cannot be confused with a real one": the Greek letter lower case pi.

4. If the final leaf in every known copy of a book is missing and the text is complete, the missing leaf may even have been used in some other book, and it may be best to give the collation "as we actually find it"—e.g. A-Y^6, Z^5.

5. Preliminary matter was generally printed last, sometimes as part of the final gathering—e.g. *^{2}, A-Y^4, Z^2. *^{1},A-Y^4, Z^3. In each of these cases, gathering Z and gathering * were printed together on a large sheet of paper containing four leaves.

Reference (McKerrow)

6. $ could be "understood to stand for any signature whatever;" thus "$3, 4 unsigned except D" could mean that "the third and fourth leaves of every gathering were unsigned, except D which was signed throughout."

7. 2B could stand for BB, 3b for bbb; thus leaf 3K2 would probably be actually signed KKK2.

8. Leaves are "usually referred to by the arabic number"—e.g. a leaf signed BBiii would be referred to as 2B3.

9. A series of signatures may be repeated one or more times—e.g., a-z^4, a-h^4. Reference to a leaf in the second series might be ^{2}d4 which would mean "d4 of the second alphabet."

10. An unsigned preliminary gathering could be referred to using lower case pi.

11. An unsigned gathering inserted in the body of the book could be referred to using lower case chi (a usage borrowed from Greg). An alternative would be to use the preceding letter with a plus sign; "thus D+2 would indicate the second leaf of an unsigned gathering following D. This . . . has the advantage of showing at once the exact position of the insertion." Or, if D has four leaves, the reference might be D4+2 (also borrowed from Greg).

12. If a leaf is itself unsigned, though forming part of a signed gathering "it is usual" to use brackets—e.g. [B8v].

McKerrow made only suggestions; he did not lay down laws. At every point he deferred to usage. Even so, he now and then moved toward jargon: it is not, for instance, certain that among real collation signatures which include *, &, and the picture of a hand, a Greek letter such as pi or chi "cannot be confused with a real" signature (No. 3); it is even less certain that the reader would understand what the Greek letter signified. Nor is it likely that the reference word saving (6 words instead of 16) produced by the sign $ in No. 6 justifies the time demanded of the reader to puzzle out its meaning. Finally, "^{2}d4" (No. 9) is not dramatically better than "d4 of the second alphabet" or (say) "[2d]d4".

A number of McKerrow's suggestions had come from Greg. Greg published his own somewhat more elaborate "Formulary of Collation" in *Library* 4th ser. 14(1934)365-382. He called his ideas "notes" and he aimed only at "stating and defining the common practice of bibliographers." Although he was setting down the method he himself used, he had "not the least wish to impose or press it upon any one else."

Greg's "Formulary" leaned heavily on McKerrow; but in a number of cases he elaborated on McKerrow or differed from him, or even introduced something entirely new. A few examples are summarized below. (The numbering is my own.)

Reference (considered first by Greg)

1. A reference to (say) D applies to the gathering, not to D1. D1r (or simply D1) means D1 recto; D1v means D1 verso.

2. An "inferential signature" may be within brackets—e.g. [C8] but "we can indicate it more neatly . . . as *C*8." (Cf. McKerrow No. 12.)

3. The Symbol $ might be used to mean *any* signature as well as *every* signature." (Cf. McKerrow No. 6.)

4. $1, 4 indicates individual leaves; $1.4 indicates conjugate leaves.

5. A(o) indicates the outer form of sheet A; A(i) indicates the inner form. If the gathering consists of more than one sheet one could write, for instance, A 2.5(o) and A 2.5(i).

Statement (Greg)

6. The number of leaves in a gathering is indicated by an "index" number after the signature letter; "thus if the signatures of a quire run $1-8 we write $^{8} and so on." (McKerrow No. 1 had called it a "superior" figure.)

7. We may write 2a in place of aa and 2A in place of AA or Aa. (Cf. McKerrow No. 7.)

8. A-Z^4 2A-2Z^4 3A-3K^4 may be written simply A-3K^4.

9. Arbitrary signs may be treated as if they were "alphabets of

one letter only." Thus ** may be called 2* and the series *, **, ***, **** in fours may be written *-4*^{4}.

10. A book with gatherings in fours signed A-K and A-V would be described A-K^4, ^{2}A-V^4. (Cf. McKerrow No. 9.)

11. If the signatures run in three series (e.g., A-2C^4 A-X^4 A-3K^4) the statement would be: A-2C^4 ^{2}A-X^4 ^{3}A-3K^4.

12. An unsigned preliminary gathering may receive "the inferential signature" A within brackets or "as I prefer" in italics—e.g. [A]^4 B-K^4 or A^4 B-K^4. (Cf. Greg No. 2 and McKerrow No. 12.)

13. Preliminary unsigned gatherings without "inferential signatures" may be referred to using Greek lower case pi. Unsigned gatherings within the book may be referred to using Greek lower case chi. (Cf. McKerrow No. 3, No. 10, and No. 11.)

14. As to commas in the statement (such as McKerrow had used): "Any lavish use is to be deprecated. One occasionally sees formulas hirsute with commas merely bewildering." Greg would use commas only "before a duplicated alphabet"—e.g., A-K^4, ^{2}A-V^4—and "to mark off any incomplete alphabet" —e.g., A-K^4, 2A-V^4.

15. The index number should always be an even number. If a leaf has been suppressed, it may be shown $4 (-$3); if a leaf has been added, $4($3+1).

16. Cancels are recorded as "suppression *plus* addition"— e.g., $4 ($\pm$$3) if a single leaf replaces a single leaf; $4 (-$3+2) if two leaves replace one.

And so on and on. Greg correctly protested that he had dealt with only "the more usual abnormalities"; if any were to complain that he had "elaborated convention beyond the limits of convenience" he could but plead that he had "only introduced fresh notations to meet actual needs and not of malice prepense." In any event, as we have noted, Greg had "not the least wish to impose or press it upon any one else." Years later, when Greg wrote his "Excursus IV" on formulas of collation (vol. 4, cxlviii-clviii), he stated that he had followed "with little variation the system" set forth in his "Formulary"; and he explained it again.

Perhaps a series of difficult devices in collation statements is not harmful if the inventor has no wish to "press it upon any one else" and if he explains it in the introduction of the bibliography in which he uses it.

But Bowers would tolerate no such nonsense. If bibliographical description is to be "normally intelligible in every detail to a reader," there must be a "standard and universal system of notation . . . adopted by all writers, at least in English-speaking countries." First, however, "two opposed schools of thought must be reconciled": One school would make "the ubiquitous 'general reader' . . . able to understand the description without special instruction" by being "less concise" and using "descriptive phrasing instead of arbitrary symbols." The second school of thought would try to be "as concise and precise as possible by the use of various symbols and shorthand practices with the significance of which a reader must be familiar." But the "nontechnical school cannot, from a scholarly point of view" be supported because of the "superior qualifications of technical symbols" in collation. Indeed, the "hypothetical 'general reader' is either a myth or in such a minority as a user of the technical parts of bibliographical description" that his needs should not outweigh "the convenience of the more numerous specialized readers." The use that such a general reader could make of the information in "bibliographical collations" is "somewhat dubious" because that information "concerns the method of printing, which must in turn be beyond this general reader's understanding" (26-27).

Thus firmly the two schools were "reconciled." In any event, "the characters employed in standard description are very few and readily learned" (28). To prove it he offered two collation statements for John Evelyn's *Sylva* (1664).

The General Reader statement requires 126 letters and other characters; the Shorthand Notation, 46—roughly one-third as many. In a printed bibliography the space used by collation statement and reference to it for each entry is a relatively small part of the total space required for that entry; it may be that the space saved by shorthand notation is more apparent than real (see also *Library Quarterly* 21[1951]62-63).

The chief problem is that a "standard and universal system of notation . . . adopted by all writers" demands a ready-made description of the result of every variation that may ever occur in the printing and publishing of any book anywhere any time. Vigorously and valiantly and vainly Bowers tilted at this wind-mill, drawing on every detail of his own vast experience. McKer-row's eight pages had blossomed into Greg's eighteen pages. Bowers waxed encyclopedic: Format and Collational Formula, 193-254. Interlude: Reference Notation, 255-268. Collational Formula Line (Incunabula), 332-338. Collational Formula (19th-20th Century Books), 431-434. A Digest of the Formulary, 457-462. All this to explain the "very few and readily learned" characters used "in standard description."

Actually, with Bowers as with McKerrow and Greg, the unusual characters confronting the uninitiated user were indeed "very few and readily learned": two Greek letters, the dollar sign, the initial superior figure, the italic inferential signature, the combined plus and minus sign. Only six mystic symbols. But the problems these figures were invented to represent come up again and again in an infinite variety of combinations.

4. *The Country Cousin*

In the hierarchy of Bibliography the cataloger stands lowest of the low. Catalogers are, proclaimed Bowers, unskilled con-structors of "catch-alls of undigested raw material" whose "loose standards" are "adjusted to the capabilities of personnel engaged in mass production" and "may not require examination of a book by a person competent to decide between a press-corrected and a cancellans title-page" (49, n. 8 and BSA *Papers* 42[1948]343). Catalogers may be all of that. And yet . . . Bib-liography, we have suggested, is the study of books as physical objects. The cataloger, among other duties—many other duties—*describes* books as physical objects; and to that extent he, no less than the bibliographer, performs a bibliographical service. The bibliographer, on the other hand, describes *and interprets* books as physical objects. It would be interesting to know how many of the examples of intricate printing and publishing history which crowd Bowers' pages are the result of interpretive studies undertaken by a bibliographer because some cataloger had noted and described in his catalog an unusual feature in a book which he had not himself the time to analyze.

Again, the bibliographer writes for publication in a printed bibliography or in an article in a bibliographical journal. When he calls a particular form of a book an "issue" or when he writes a collation of that book using a particular formulary, he can state clearly in the introduction to his bibliography or in the context of his article precisely how and why he uses the term or constructs the collation. Everybody knows what he means and no harm has been done.

But when the word "issue" or a particular collation statement appears in a checklist catalog, or a bookseller's catalog, or a card catalog, the case is different. There the term "issue" and the collation must stand alone with little or no interpretation. There, rather than in the printed bibliography or in the printed article, the "accurate and precise transmission of bibliographical meaning" (Bowers in BSA *Papers* 41[1947]271) rests upon the use of the word. Many more books are recorded in such catalogs than in printed bibliographies and learned bibliographical articles; and, until such books have been analyzed and described by bibliographers, these brief catalog entries are the only descriptions available to scholars. There is, thus, much less cross reference between printed bibliographies than between printed bibliographies and catalogs or between catalogs and other catalogs.

How do we make this cross reference meaningful and easy? We return to the three things a bibliographer tells about a book he has examined as a physical object (p. 13 above); (1) Classification, (2) Transcription, and (3) Collation. How does the cataloger deal with them? There have been two books on rare book cataloging and at least one important article: J. D. Cowley, *Bibliographical Description and Cataloguing* (1949); Paul S. Dunkin, *How to Catalog a Rare Book* (2d ed., rev. 1973); and John E. Alden, "Cataloging and Classification" in *Rare Book Collections,* edited by H. Richard Archer (1965)65-73. Also there are the American Library Association rules for general cataloging. Each will be noted where appropriate below.

1. *Classification.* Because the cataloger merely describes, he can use only words of description; for this reason, "issue" also must be a word used to describe a combination of details rather than to interpret them. To the cataloger the differences among books are simply differences; they are not changes made by any particular person for any particular reason at any particular time in the history of the book's production and sale. He finds in books two kinds of differences: (1) differences which set apart a group of books from another group of books, and (2) differences which set apart a particular book from other books in the group to which it belongs. A setting of type is a difference of the first kind; it sets apart one "edition" from another. Within the major group called an "edition" there may be smaller groups marked by title page differences and/or additions and important textual differences elsewhere and/or cancellations in any part of the book. What the cataloger calls these subgroups does not greatly matter to him but he tends to call them "issues" and to identify them by their differences rather than by the single word "issue." Press corrections are differences of the second type. The cataloger normally ignores them, but when he calls the book they set apart anything it is usually "state" or "variant." In general, this is the attitude explained by Dunkin; Cowley, Alden, and ALA rules ignore classification.

2. *Transcription.* Here, perhaps, cataloger and bibliographer come closest together. Cowley described quasi-facsimile, but he endorsed a full transcription in roman lower case using capitals only when necessary, and indicating line endings and omissions. Generally speaking, the cataloger has favored long titles even for ordinary books, but he has seldom bothered with line endings or different kinds of type. Wide use of Library of Congress catalog cards and close attention to the detailed ALA codes have worked for standardization of elaborate transcription. Alden endorsed most ALA practices for rare book cataloging. There was, indeed, one inquiry into the underlying logic of full transcription in cataloging (the Library of Congress *Studies*

noted above on page 20), but catalogers have never seriously
tried to use the brief transcription which the LC *Studies* showed
would be adequate to identify edition and issues. Dunkin tried
to show that the LC *Studies* along with the two other studies
noted above (pages 20-21) seem to mean that transcription even
for rare books could be very brief indeed.

The International Standard Bibliographic Description (1971)
differed from all earlier rules primarily in that it employs standard "punctuation," unlike anything else ever defined as "punctuation" between fields and subfields of the description—marks
that are unique in these positions so that the process of coding
these elements can be mechanized. The marks include the point
and dash (.—) to separate each area from the next; the equals
sign (=) to separate parallel titles from the title proper; and the
diagonal slash (/) to separate statements of authorship from
the title(s) or edition statement. As the cataloger adopts *ISBD*
he moves dangerously away from all other bibliographers, and,
indeed, dangerously away from the user because he seeks first to
accommodate the capabilities of the machine. *Anglo-American
Cataloging Rules, Chapter 6* (rev. 1974) adopted *ISBD*.

3. *Collation.* For most books the cataloger depends on a statement of pagination alone (usually the last numbered page or leaf
of each paged section) with no reference to collation by gatherings. The LC *Studies* showed that pagination is in many cases
enough to separate editions and issues. On the other hand, the
cataloger of a rare book must collate that book by gatherings if
he is to be sure that he has what seems to be the entire book. The
cost of adding this collation by gatherings to his entry is only the
cost of the clerical time of the typist who copies his statement.
Alden suggested the addition of collation by gatherings. Cowley
endorsed Greg's "Formulary". Dunkin suggested a collation
derived from the signatures used in the book with problems set
forth clearly and simply in conventional (rather than "short-
hand") words and devices—e.g., instead of the Greek letters for
unsigned leaves or gatherings, it is generally possible to use
within brackets the signatures which the user might normally
expect:

[A]² B-P⁴.
[A]² A-P⁴.

A-G^4 [H]^2 I-P^4.
A-G^4 [H]^2 H-P^4.

Of all the bibliographers the cataloger would seem most apt to speak the language of more of the non-bibliographers who use Bibliography. Like every librarian, the cataloger is by definition a dabbler, a man who must have a smattering of all the many specialities in which his clients are interested. But he is just too busy to master any one man's jargon; he can only speak and write what he hopes is clear English and hope that what he says will help each man find the book or the bit of information he needs. The cataloger's classification of editions, issues, and state is simple; his transcription tends to be wordy, but only if he follows *ISBD* too closely is he in danger; finally, his statement of pagination and his collation by gatherings demand no passwords. All this is no virtue in the cataloger. It is only the necessary result of his way of life. He serves everyman; therefore he must use the tongue of everyman.

5. *Clutch of Door Knobs*

Classification, Transcription, Collation—in all three respects Bibliography since McKerrow has come more and more to be written by bibliographers for bibliographers. Distinctions between editions, issues, and states grow ever more intricate; elaborate transcription flourishes even alongside photographic reproduction; and collation by gatherings bristles with mystic symbols.

As to the non-bibliographer groups which bibliography can serve—textual critics, historical and other scholars, librarians— they had just better get with it and learn to speak in tongues. Particularly the librarian; if he persists in his refusal to "learn about books from the scholarly, which is to say the bibliographical, point of view," he will have "little idea of what is contained in descriptive bibliographies, because he cannot read them. He can sit on his books like a hen on a clutch of eggs, but what he hatches will be less useful. China door knobs, most likely" (Bowers, *Library Trends* 7[1959]506 and 508).

Part Two

The Great Leap

Forward ?

We have seen that over the past fifty years bibliographers have invented their own language to tell each other what they have found out about books as physical objects. What have they found out? Much indeed. They have crammed periodicals and books and they have not always agreed about what they have found.

We shall look rather closely at some of these discoveries, the explanations some bibliographers have offered, and the new questions those explanations have sometimes raised.

1. *Skeleton on the Move*

The basic unit of the book as a physical object is a gathering of leaves produced by folding a part of a large sheet of paper, a whole sheet, or several sheets. Bibliographers call the side of this large printed sheet which contains the sheet's first leaf recto (i.e., its first page) the "outer form" of the sheet; the side which contains the first leaf verso (i.e., the second page) of the large printed sheet is the "inner form." Bibliographers borrow this term "form" from printers; but to printers the "form" is not the printed side of a large sheet of paper. Instead, to printers the term "form" means the pages of type from which that side of the large sheet of paper is printed. The early printer locked the pages of type for a form into place within a rectangular iron frame called a "chase" by means of pieces of wood called "furniture." For each new form in the book he did not use a new chase and new furniture. Instead, once as many copies of one side of a large sheet as were needed had been printed, he removed the chase and furniture of the old form and placed them about the type pages of the next form, taking care to put each piece of furniture into its corresponding location in the new form so that the printed pages of the book would match. All this was described in specific detail 300 years ago in the first English printer's manual (Moxon, 229; cf. Savage, 333).

But the printer normally transferred more than just the chase and furniture from one form to the next. He also transferred the headlines, brass rules surrounding the text—anything he could use in the new form (see, for instance, printers' manuals such as those by John Smith [1755], 264; Philip Luckombe [1771], 409; Caleb Stower [1808], 163 and 207). In the printed book, breaks in the headline type, bent or broken places in the rules, other flaws—these defects betray to the bibliographer the presence of what he calls a "skeleton form," and by following the reappearances of skeleton forms throughout the book he can try to trace the history of the printing of that book.

Although A. W. Pollard noted the importance of headlines as early as 1909 (*Shakespeare Folios and Quartos*, 134-5), McKerrow did not refer to them, and the first intensive use of the headline-skeleton form phenomenon was in Willoughby's masterly *Printing of the First Folio of Shakespeare* (1932). The Folio is made up of sheets, each folded once to produce two leaves (i.e., four pages), with each gathering normally consisting of three folded sheets (i.e., six leaves or 12 pages); and the collation statement is rather involved. Among other things, Willoughby's study seemed to show that:

1. One whole play (*Winter's Tale*) was inserted after the material now preceding and following it had been printed.
2. After some twenty-five gatherings had been printed, work was interrupted for over a year while two or more other substantial books were printed.
3. Even after printing began again there were a number of irregularities and the sequence of the collation often does not reflect the sequence of the printing.

In addition to the skeleton form Willoughby used some of the other techniques discussed below, and later students were to challenge some of his conclusions; but after his book appeared in 1932, bibliographers ignored skeleton forms at their peril. Even so, Bowers found it necessary again to call attention to the study of headlines in 1938 (*Library* 4th ser. 19[1938]326-31) and in 1941 *English Institute Annual, 1941* (1942) 187. It is ironic that by 1969 McKenzie referred to the Bowers papers as "the pioneer study in the use of headlines" (*SB* 22[1969]24).

We shall look briefly at a few other studies of skeleton forms, not necessarily the chief or the best, but enough perhaps to show some trends and problems. Like the Willoughby study, most of those listed below involve other techniques in addition to the use of skeleton forms.

R. C. Bald's *Bibliographical Studies in the Beaumont & Fletcher Folio of 1647* (1938) was a book for which Willoughby's study "provided an invaluable model in bibliographical method" (v). "No less than eight different printers" (20) printed sections of the folio and in each section the skeleton forms were helpful in showing the progress of the printing, although apparently the printers had other material being printed at the same time.

Curt F. Bühler's "The Headlines of William de Machlinia's *Year-Book*, 37 Henry VI" (*SB* 1 [1948-49]125-132) was a modest attempt to "try my prentice hand at this line of investigation" and it showed nothing more than that the skeleton form could be studied in incunabula as well as in books of later times.

Similarly Stanley Boorman's "Upon the Use of Running Titles in the Aldus House in 1518" (*Library* 5th ser. 27[1972]126-131) reports only on running titles, finding that in books examined "running titles were regarded as distinct from the rest of the page, but that in a number of instances they functioned as part of the skeleton forme" (131).

Somewhat more interesting is the relationship of the skeleton form to cancels. Broadly speaking, if the sequence of skeleton forms in a book is interrupted by one or more leaves or even gatherings using a different skeleton or series of skeletons and then the first sequence takes up again with no return to the variant skeletons, the cause may be that the leaf or leaves with the different skeleton are cancels. Thus, for instance, I. A. Shapiro noted that the headlines of gathering D in *The Defence of Conny-Catching* (1592) indicate that gathering as a probable cancel (*Library* 5th ser. 18[1963]94-96). Similarly headlines seem to show that an original gathering I in Foxe's *Acts and Monuments* (1570) was cancelled by two gatherings signed I and *I* (*Library* 5th ser. 2[1947/48]168). Conversely, Bowers noted that the headlines do not suggest that cancellation caused the three-leaf gathering E in Thomas Southerne's *Disappointment* (1684) (*Library* 5th ser. 5[1950/51]140-149).

Skeleton forms may help distinguish and sometimes explain editions and issues. Beginning with sheet E of the first edition of Fletcher-Betterton *The Prophetess* (1690) a decision seems to have been made to enlarge the edition. Sheets B-D, already printed, were later reset and run with different headlines; but sheets of the rest of the book were printed to the larger number and are identical in both issues (Bowers in *Library* 5th ser. 16 [1961]169-175). On the other hand, two different groups of headlines for gathering E in Elkanah Settle's *Fairy Queen* (1692) may indicate that the printer abruptly decided to run off a small number of complete copies of the book for sale while the opera was begin presented and then to finish printing the entire edition at leisure (Willoughby in *Library* 4th ser. 26[1945/46]301-302).

"An Examination of the Method of Proof Correction in LEAR" by Bowers (*Library* 3d ser. 2[1947/48]20-44) was written in response to a theory of the method of taking proof in early books developed by Greg without study of skeleton forms. Bowers' solution, based on study of headlines in *Lear* (1608) may be correct, but it may also not be as important as two problems it raises.

One is the sequence of headlines as they were used in skeleton

forms. Moxon was quite specific on this point (229-30). From
the form just printed the compositor "takes off the chase, and
lays it about those pages he is imposing: then with his two fore-
fingers and thumbs he takes away the inner side-stick and the
head-stick [i.e., furniture at the inner and top margins of the
type page] at once, and at once removes them to the responding
quarter of the form imposing, into the responding places from
whence he took them in the wrought off form. And as he does by
the inner side-sticks, so he does by the outer side-sticks [i.e., furniture at the other margins] and by the quoins [wedges used to
lock up the form]; placing them in their respective proper places
between the furniture and chase. . . . Thus the wrought off
form is stript and naked; and stands by to distribute."

Bowers called attention to this statement (26), but the Moxon
sequence of transfer is not the sequence suggested by Bowers for
Lear (27): Beginning with sheet D, "the customary way in which
the type pages for $1-2v [i.e., 1 recto, 1 verso, 2 recto, 2 verso of
each gathering—a total of four pages] are imposed from a
wrought-off forme of a sheet once removed in printing, indicates
that when the compositor had set $2v he customarily stripped an
available rinsed forme and imposed its quarters about the first
two pages of both formes which had been set and placed in imposing position on the stone. Thus D1-2v are imposed from the
skeleton of B(i) [i.e., the inner form of gathering B]; E1-2v from
C(o) [i.e., the outer form of gathering C]; G1-2v from E (i); H1-2v
from F (i).

"The most obvious and, I believe, the correct explanation
is that Okes [the printer] ordinarily needed the type in the
wrought-off forme before he composed type-page $4, and that
he adopted this unusual expedient to free it for distribution."

The headlines used with D1r, D1v, D2r, and D2v (Bowers' first
example) are numbered by Bowers VI, VIII, VII, and IX respectively and he states that these headlines reappear in the book in
the following sequences (21-22):

VI B2r D1r F1r *G3v* I3v L1v
VIII B4r *D1v E3r* F4r H2r *K2v*
VII B1v *D2r F1v H1r* I4r
  IX B3v D2v E4v F4v *G4v I2v* K1v L3v

We now return to Moxon and his emphasis on getting the furniture from one form exactly into a corresponding position in the form being imposed. On any leaf of almost any book the inner and outer margins of the recto are the reverse of the corresponding verso margins; that is, the left margin of the recto is narrow and the right margin is wide while the left margin of the verso is wide and the right is narrow. The arrangement of the furniture creating these margins would not be interchangeable. (See Gaskell Fig. 43 and 44.) In a quarto form such as printed each side of a large sheet in *Lear* there are two rectos and two versos; this may be seen in the pages of the inner form of B listed in the first column above: B1v, B2r, B3v, B4r. Apparently this is the reason for Moxon's insistence that furniture be moved from one form to the "responding" place in the new form. But the Bowers table above shows that this did not happen in *Lear* if the headlines are any indication. The headlines of inner B, for instance, fail to move into corresponding position in a later form; instead, they are divided between two forms (outer and inner D). Even more: B4 recto headline moves to D1 *verso* and B1 verso headline moves to D2 *recto* instead of to corresponding recto and verso pages already available in D. During the printing of the rest of the book each of these four headlines moves now and then from a recto position to a verso position or from a verso position to a recto position; in the table above each such move is indicated by italicizing the page on which the change occurred. All other headlines in the book move from one page to another with a similar disregard for recto and verso.

If the headlines in *Lear* represent "quarters" of skeleton forms, it seems probable that these "quarters" were frequently moved to new forms only by taking time to change the furniture to positions other than those "responding" to positions in the old form; in one case at least (B4r and B1v) this troublesome switch was deliberately chosen (see above). Perhaps the headlines, then, were detached from the skeleton forms and moved independently of them.

In any event, Bowers' solution was derived only from study of the headlines, ignoring Moxon's explicit statement and the underlying logic which that statement seems to infer. Neglect of Moxon and other printing manuals is not peculiar to Bowers;

much of what bibliographers have written has been based only on the examination of the physical book and what they could infer from that examination.

A second problem shows up at various places. Consider some of Bowers' criticisms of Greg's theory: "It is clear that the press must have been idle during the time that outer D was rinsed, stripped, and parts of its skeleton imposed about the type-pages of inner E. Since such delays would cost Okes money if they happened during the printing day, we should expect them to be cut to a minimum" (23). "We should need to believe that the compositor five times did not take the short-cut of utilizing already-rinsed formes which were available but went out of his way to rinse immediately a forme just off the press and to strip its skeleton to the new type-pages before completing his imposition" (25). "With one skeleton printing there is nothing for the press to work on when the forme is removed for correction" (29). "It constructs an elaborate process requiring three skeletons to save time by simultaneous imposition of two formes, but the evidence of the headlines shows that any time saved was squandered in excess by delays in presswork between all but two sheets consequent upon the simultaneous imposition" (41). On the other hand, Bowers' suggested method of proofing "provides for only three breaks in continuous presswork. . . . The explanation is perhaps suspiciously neat, but if it is right, there was never any actual delay in continuous presswork throughout the entire book" (42).

Behind all these statements lie two assumptions:

1. *Lear* was the only project Okes and his men worked on during the time of its printing. This may have been true, but there is no proof. Indeed, Willoughby and Bald found printers working with more than one book at a time. Printers' records of the eighteenth century reflect concurrent production as common practice (see below, p. 80-81). Moreover, there may have been job work from time to time (cf. P. M. Handover, *Printing in London from 1476 to Modern Times* [1960] 172-195).

2. Okes was a careful, time-saving planner who made every minute count. He may, indeed, have been just that. Or he may have been only an ordinary mortal—sometimes careful, some-

times careless; sometimes in a hurry, sometimes slow; sometimes calculating, sometimes emotional. If we accept the Bowers skeletons, Okes or one of his men chose to take the time to transpose the furniture of B4r about the type of D1v and the furniture of B1v about the type of D2r when he could simply have transferred the furniture of B4r intact as it stood to D2r and B1v to D1v. One of the intriguing qualities of Moxon is the elaborate detail with which he describes every motion of the printer (see the passage quoted above). But it seems possible that Moxon's motive was simply didactic—not a wish to do a time and motion study.

These two assumptions underlie almost every study of the movement of skeleton forms.

There are at least three other problems with the study of skeleton forms: 1. It takes a lot of time, particularly if the book is thick or has a complicated format. Bowers, nonetheless, suggests that the bibliographical examination of a book is complete only if every headline has been identified and every variation in its use explained (*English Institute Annual 1941* [1942]188). 2. Frequently, as with Bühler above (p. 37) nothing unusual appears; yet only with the study can we be sure. 3. It is useful only with early printing; by the eighteenth century headlines are hard to distinguish.

2. Casting Off for What?

We begin with Moxon (239): "Counting or casting off copy (for both phrases are indifferently us'd) is to examine and find how much either of printed copy will come-in into any intended number of sheets of a different body or measure from the copy; or how much written copy will make an intended number of sheets of any assigned body and measure." His details last through p. 244.

Many years later William Savage's *Dictionary of the Art of Printing* (1841) was more concise: "CASTING UP. Calculating the number of thousands of letters in a sheet of any work, or in a job, in order to fix the price for composing it." He then gave a long set of tables "useful to those compositors who are not expert at figures".

W. H. Bond described marks made by the printer in a manuscript of 1508 (*SB* 8[1956]147-156):

The marks "were, as one might expect, on a severely practical level. First of all, he cast off the copy to determine how many pages of print it would occupy. Probably by experiment he found that forty-nine lines of manuscript produced about one page (forty-two lines) of printing; so one of his first acts was to mark the manuscript every seventh line, that being the common denominator of these two figures. . . . The entire manuscript, with very few exceptions, was so marked"(155).

"The manuscript was also marked to show the division into pages of type . . . and in the margin was written the number of the page within the particular quire which began at that point. . . . Some of these marks appear to represent experimental casting-off or else trial settings, where as many as three divisions appear for each page. In these cases, all but the mark for the eventual division are deleted by crossing out" (155).

But there could be more to casting off than just calculating prospective cash; and McKerrow, although he gave no example, cited (34) Moxon's hint: "But no wise compositor, except he work on printed copy that runs sheet for sheet, will be willing to compose more sheets to a quire than he shall have a fount of letter large enough to set out, unless he will take upon him the trouble of counting off his copy; because he cannot impose till he has set to the last page of that quire; all the other sheets being quired within the first sheet, and the last page of the quire comes in the first sheet" (Moxon 210-211).

By "quire" Moxon meant what is above called a "gathering" and he is here writing of a folio gathering composed of more than one large sheet. If, for instance, we had a gathering made up of three large sheets each folded once, it would be a folio gathering consisting of six leaves (twelve pages). The leaf carrying page 1 and page 2 would be conjugate with the leaf carrying pages 11 and 12. (Perhaps this will be more easily understood if the reader will fold three sheets of typing paper one time across the short fold and place the second sheet inside the first and the third inside the second; this will result in a comparable gathering.)

If the compositor setting type to print such a gathering begins with page 1, then sets page 2, then page 3, and so on, he will not have a complete form capable of printing two pages till he has set pages 6 and 7; this means he will have 7 pages of type immobilized before he can start printing. If, however, he (to use Moxon's phrase) "will take upon him the trouble of counting off his copy," then he can set (say) page 1 and page 12 and at once begin printing this outer form of the outer sheet while composition on the form for (say) page 2 and page 11 goes ahead with no great strain on the type supply.

One of Hinman's major contributions seems to have been the discovery that the Shakespeare First Folio (largely in 6-leaf gatherings) was set and printed by forms instead of by successive pages. Proof lay in the fact that certain distinctive types recur "in pages of a single quire where impressions from the same actual type could certainly not be found" if composition had been by successive pages (I, 56). Hinman identified "some 600-odd individually distinctive types" and tabulated their appearance and reappearance in the book. Apparently the innermost form of the gathering was normally the first to be set and imposed and the outermost form the last.

Unlike Moxon, Hinman suggested an economic reason (rather than type shortage) for casting off. "Casting off copy would make possible the simultaneous setting of different Folio pages by different compositors. Hence Jaggard might well have undertaken it even if his supplies of type had been unlimited" (I,74). The time ratio between composing and printing, Hinman felt, "could be effected and effected economically, if two compositors worked simultaneously on its various formes—and Jaggard probably cast off the copy for it with precisely this end in view" (I,75). Composition-presswork time ratio is, of course, a tricky business; there are so many variables such as size of edition, size and kind of type, other work possibly being done at the same time. Skeleton forms, recurrence of distinctive types, and the like may, indeed, indicate something of the sequence of forms being printed, but "the same *sequence* may be followed at variable *speeds*" (McKenzie 34, n.63). Moxon's reason remains sound: "more sheets to a quire than he shall have a fount of letter large enough to set out."

Casting off copy for prose should be more difficult than casting off for poetry or plays largely in verse because in verse the line endings are already determined; on the other hand, detecting it in prose should be more easy. William H. Bond tackled the problem in his "Casting off Copy by Elizabethan Printers: a Theory" (BSA *Papers* 42[1948]281-291). In five octavos printed by Thomas Marshe, in a quarto published by Ralph Newberry and Henry Bynneman, and in a quarto printed by Thomas Creede, he found irregularity in the number of lines to the page. Generally this irregularity occurs in pages of the inner forms, and seldom in both forms of any one gathering. In several books it is obvious that the two forms of a gathering cannot have been imposed concurrently—e.g., in his first example only one set of headlines (that is, only one skeleton form) was used throughout. Apparently with each of these books the printer seems to have (1) Cast off copy for printing by forms; (2) Generally set and printed each outer form before its companion inner form; and (3) Sometimes found that he had left too much or too little copy for an inner form and crammed or spaced out its pages of type accordingly. Presumably the reason for casting off was shortage of type. In spite of Bond's modest disclaimer that "all this is merely theory" (290), his theory seems convincing.

George Walton Williams examined several books printed by Thomas Creede in his "Setting by Formes in Quarto Printing" (*SB* 11[1958]39-53). The first is a single sheet quarto containing verse in twelve-line stanzas set three to a page. His chief evidence lies in the compositor's use of the letter "w" and its substitute "vv" as shown in the following table:

	A1v	A2r	A3v	A4r	A2v	A3r	A4v	A1r
w		20	26	15	19	3		
vv						30		1

Williams contends that if the type pages were set in natural sequence, the use of w and vv would be chaotic; for A3r, for instance, the compositor used w 3 times and vv 30 times— apparently because w was exhausted—only to return to w 26 times on the next page A3v. But, with type pages arranged by forms, he finds a pattern of use of w throughout the inner form (A1v, A2r, A3v, A4r) continued into the outer form beginning with A2v and ending on A3r with use of vv beginning on A3r where w leaves off and continuing through A4v (where there is neither w nor vv) into A1r (the title page) with 1 vv. This pattern, he suggests, is evidence that the pamphlet was set and printed by forms.

Such evidence, however, seems to raise some questions:

1. It rests on the assumption that "the compositor was not indifferent to the w/vv distinction" because on A3r "the proper forms appear at the top of the page and the substitute forms follow them" (41)—although Williams hastens to explain in footnote 6 that actually only two w sorts appear at the top of A3r and the third comes in line 14 after 9vv forms, "clearly a piece that has been misplaced and was discovered . . . in time to be set in the middle of the page." "Clearly" only if we accept the Williams theory.

2. If the compositor truly preferred w, it is sad to find that he ended up with a vv on his title page (A1r). Apparently it did not occur to him to begin setting his outer form with A1; with a simple two-form book and copy already cast off there would be little need to set the title page last. Nor, apparently, did it occur to him to trade his vv on A1r for a w on A2v or A3r (both in the same form as A1r).

3. If the pages had been set in normal sequence, the fact that A3r with its w 3 times and vv 30 times was followed by A3v with w 26 times could mean merely that at this point type from another job had been distributed restoring the w supply. Williams contends, however, that "a distribution of type in the midst of" so small a work "would have been improbable" (42). "Improbable" only if we assume that this one-sheet pamphlet was the only thing going in Creede's shop at the time. Williams uses this same kind of type-shortage evidence to show setting by

forms in other books, but twice (43 and 45) he explains away breaks in the shortage pattern by distribution of "type used in earlier press work."

4. McKenzie (38) remarks on Williams' willingness to accept "random mixing of roman and italic forms of k, K, S, and Q" as "common" and "without significance" in another book whereas the "shortage of lower case w . . . discloses a pattern throughout the quarto" (Williams 42-43). Mixing of roman and italic K, however, may not be comparable with mixing of w and vv. Roman and italic K might be in the same box in the case because of careless (or deliberate) distribution, but w and v in the same box would delay the compositor wanting only v or only w. Nor would any "pattern" in the use of w and v be for aesthetic reasons (No. 1 and No. 2 above); instead it would simply be the mechanical result of the fact that the compositor would use up every thing in the w box before he moved to the v box because the v box would cause him to set two pieces of type (instead of one) for one letter.

George R. Price wrote about "Setting by Formes in the First Edition of *The Phoenix*" (BSA *Papers* 56[1962]414-427). The book has collation A-I⁴ K², and "the most striking sort of evidence" appears in the 73 variants "distributed fairly evenly among the four pages" of the outer form of B in the Harvard copy (415).

Price thought that the reason for so many errors "may be implicit in the *fact* that outer B was composed as a test of the accuracy of cast-off copy. *Probably* the compositor actually intended . . . rapidly to test the casting off and, second to correct the forme before printing began. But for some reason he forgot the correction. We may *imagine* that . . . the first few pulls were made before a pressman noticed the absurd running title *The Paenix*. . . . The first stage of fifty-six corrections followed" (419). The italics in this passage are my own: nowhere has Price established a "fact"; then "fact" becomes "probably"; and we may, indeed, "imagine" almost anything. Finally, how can an unusual number of corrections in a form prove anything about casting off?

He found another bit of evidence in the initial letters of the speech heads because "bibliographers have demonstrated that the employment of roman capitals as initials" of italic speech heads "generally shows the depletion of the compositor's font of italic." So he suggested this probable order of composition: (1) outer B with 44 italic and 9 roman capitals; (2) inner B with 21 italic and 37 roman; (3) inner A with 5 italic and 14 roman; and (4) outer A with 10 italic and 27 roman. "The remaining formes" do not show such a pattern "for it would seem that the compositor in his distribution of type did not constantly maintain a complete separation of the two fonts of capitals" (422-423). But why are there *any* italics in inner B if outer B had exhausted the supply? Did the assumed casting off by forms cease after gathering B? Would failure to "maintain a complete separation of the two fonts" also explain the italic-roman situation in A and B?

Additional evidence, he suggested, is that "six scattered pages have a length of thirty-five lines of type instead of the normal thirty-six of this book"; five of them, he said, can be explained by faulty casting off (presumably such as occurred in the Bond examples above) while one (E1v) seems to be short because of an omitted line (423). B3r, however, is also short (417), although italic-roman capitals suggest its form (outer B) was the first form printed (see above), and in casting off and printing by forms irregularity in the number of lines to a page generally occurs in the second form set and printed because its text must be adjusted to unset copy left by the first form printed (see above with regard to the Bond article). Apparently Price believed that correction caused this short page, although he suggested that "by a miscalculation in his rapid casting off of these two pages" the original compositor "ended with a shortage of two lines at the foot of B3r" (417). Finally there is the puzzling earlier remark: "In all but eight scattered pages of this edition, the type pages reach thirty-six lines" (417). Do we have two short pages unaccounted for?

In "The Printing of Beaumont and Fletcher's *The Maid's Tragedy* Q1 (1619)" (*SB* 13[1960]199-220), Robert K. Turner, Jr., urged that setting was by forms on the evidence of "shortage of the small capitals chosen for setting the speech-prefixes as well as of certain sorts in the roman font used for the text of the play"

(203). The discussion, however, is marred by "restrictive economic framework" and "occasional appeals to general presuppositions" (D. F. McKenzie, *Library* 5th ser. 16[1961]66).
Consider the following sentences:

1. "Under ideal conditions a compositor should have been able to set and distribute about four type pages in the same amount of time required by the press to machine one forme . . ." (204). Surely the time used by the compositor would depend on several things such as legibility of copy, kind of type being set, the compositor's own skill and speed. On the other hand, the time for press work would depend, among other variables, on how many copies were being printed and whether the press was being used only for this particular work.

2. If gathering B was set by forms (instead of by successive pages), "it must be assumed that the type used in another book was distributed between the setting of B4v and B1v. If this assumption is allowed, it is seen that a clear pattern of depletion and resupply of the larger letter emerges" (204). True, but a similar assumption might help explain irregularities with the type-supply pattern of assumed setting by successive pages (203).

3. "It should be mentioned that there is no clear line of division between the use of the large type and the small on pages where the two are mixed. . . . The more-or-less random mixture of the two sizes on certain pages would indicate only that the compositor did not completely exhaust his supply of large type before replenishing his stock with the small" (204-205). Perhaps it might also indicate that the compositor was indifferent to the use of large type or small, and/or that both sizes had been distributed into the same box.

Later Turner was to write that "By itself the testimony of shortages is, I believe, less reliable than that of any other bibliographical technique" (*SB* 15[1962]39).

Turner also studied the reappearances of recognizable types as evidence of setting by forms. "Type from distributed formes of *A King and No King* Q1 normally reappears in both formes of the succeeding sheet; in a quarto set by formes, type from the first forme of each sheet normally reappears in both formes of the succeeding sheet, but type from the second forme only in the

second forme of the succeeding sheet" (*SB* 18[1965]257-258) and
he cited as proof a passage in his study of *Midsummer Night's
Dream* Q1 (*SB* 15[1962]33-55): "Composition cannot have been
seriatim. Had it been so, B(o) . . . could not have been made
ready for the press until B4v had been set. The workman would
then have started on sheet C, but . . . B(o) had been worked off
and distributed before he reached line 5 of C1v, that is, after
he had set only a page of the new forme" because Turner considered a type on C1v, line 5, identical with a type on [B(o)]
B4v, line 24. "Presumably B(i) would then have perfected its
sheet, but this forme too was distributed during the setting of
sheet C. The press, then, would have been delayed for at least
the length of time required to set C3v and C4 before the first
forme of C could have been imposed" because types on C3v and
C4r had previously been used in B(i) on B2r and B4r respectively.
"It seems clear, then, that B(o) was completely set and sent to
the press before B(i), that it was machined and ready for distribution before the composition of C(o) was begun, that B(i)
was off the press and distributed during the setting of C(i)—in
short, that the book generally was set by formes" (36). "That
B(o) was machined in the time required to set the four type
pages of B(i) or perhaps even a little less time is indicated by its
distribution before the composition of C began. Thus the speed
of the press, which barring accidents would have remained
fairly constant, is established as the rate at which about four
type pages could be composed" (46).

   "It seems clear" and "the speed of the press . . . is established" if we assume that (1) this was the only work being done
in the shop and (2) men and press moved like clock work.

   We may be on firmer ground with D. F. McKenzie's "Eight
Quarto Proof Sheets of 1594 Set by Formes: *A fruitfull commentarie*" (*Library* 5th ser. 28[1973]1-13). Here, as with the
Shakespeare First Folio, we have a series of gatherings each of
them composed of more than one large folded sheet. The typical
Shakespeare Folio gathering consists of three sheets each folded
once (six folio leaves); *A Fruitfull Commentarie* typical gathering consists of two sheets each folded twice and one placed
inside the other (eight quarto leaves). As with the Shakespeare,

setting in the sequence of the pages would have meant no form could be printed till after the inner form of the inner sheet (a total of eleven pages) was ready to go. McKenzie's evidence of setting by forms is of three kinds:

1. *Recurrent sorts*: "The same sort could not appear more than once within the first eleven pages" of a gathering "if they were set *seriatim*. . . . But types from D3r do reappear on D2r. . . . In this case the outer forme of the innermost sheet (D3r, 4v-5r, 6v) had been printed and its type distributed before earlier pages in the gathering were set" (2).
2. *Type shortage*—e.g., there are no italic I's but 50 roman I's, in D, outer sheet, inner form, while D, outer sheet, outer form has 25 italic I's and 41 roman; apparently the compositor ran out of roman while he was setting the outer form. The inner and outer forms of the inner sheet show similar characteristics.
3. *Compression*—e.g., "The normal page depth is 40 lines, but the last two pages of forme B1v-2r, 7v-8r [B outer sheet, inner form] have 39 and 38 lines respectively" (3). "Crowding at the foot of D2v suggests that the next innermost forme (in particular page D3r) had already been set" (5).

So printers appear to have cast off copy for one of at least two reasons: (1) to determine what the price of a particular piece of work would be and/or how much paper it would require; and (2) to be able to set and print by forms rather than by gatherings in order to keep as little type as possible in use at any one time. (See also below p. 82-83). Apparently both practices had been common for many years before Moxon wrote. Evidence of casting off to set by forms is sometimes hard to come by if each gathering in a book consists of only one folded sheet; perhaps casting off to set by forms was more frequent with books in which each gathering consists of more than one folded sheet.

3. *Whodunit?*

The author did it, of course. But, like it or not, the author had helpers. We begin with Moxon (192-3):

". . . By the laws of printing, a compositor is strictly to follow his copy, viz. to observe and do just so much and no more than his copy will bear him out for; so that his copy is to be his rule and authority: but the carelessness of some good authors, and the ignorance of other authors, has forc'd printers to introduce a custom, which among them is look'd upon as a task and duty incumbent on the compositor, viz. to discern and amend the bad spelling and pointing of his copy, if it be English. . . . Therefore . . . it is necessary that a compositor be a good English schollar at least; and that he know the present traditional spelling of all English words, and that he have so much sence and reason, as to point his sentences properly: when to begin a word with a capital letter, when (to render the sence of the author more intelligent to the reader) to set some words or sentences in Italick or English letters &c."

Probably Moxon was simply stating what had long been the practice of compositors. Certainly the same approach shows up time and again in the printer's manuals which came after him.

How tell the work of one author's helper from that of another? McKerrow had two suggestions (128-29):

"It is occasionally possible to infer, from differences in spelling and in minor details of style in different parts of a book, that more than one compositor has been engaged upon it, and this may be of importance if we are considering the extent to which an author's spelling has been retained in the printed text. . . . Occasionally . . . it appears that the MS. was divided between different compositors . . . who would then work on different parts of it simultaneously. . . . The usual indication of such division . . . is that the parts do not follow one another in the normal manner."

Books in McKerrow's second group (division of copy) are easy to identify; they are also relatively few. Many bibliographers have worked with the first device: analysis of spelling. T. H. Hill drew up eight "principles for the bibliographical examination of early seventeenth-century English spelling" (*Library* 5th ser., 18[1963]1-28):

1. Elizabethan and Jacobean spelling was variable; consequently, everyone could have had his own spelling-habit.
2. Countervailing influences had the effect of establishing an Elizabethan and early seventeenth-century "standard usage." (Such influences were spelling reformers, school teachers, and printing house practices.)
3. Standard usage, however modified, was conventional rather than rational; it had little internal consistency. Each spelling-habit manifested a similar inconsistency.
4. The Elizabethan and Jacobean compositor (and copyist) followed the substance of his copy, but not the accidentals, including spelling.
5. The compositor nevertheless adopted certain spellings of his copy-text.
6. A compositorial spelling-pattern can be isolated in any text; similarly, evidence of a writer's spelling-pattern, when known from his holograph, can be isolated in a transcription, either written or printed, of it.
7. A spelling-pattern isolated in one text should also be able to be isolated in any other text for which there is reason to assume the same scribe, author, or compositor.
8. Any spelling-pattern was liable to (or subject to) modification over a period of years . . . on the other hand, spelling-habits tended to become fixed as the individual became older.

Such a set of "principles" is a twisting path through a murky swamp. Yet this path is all that the bibliographer has to follow and sometimes it seems to lead to a clear vision such as Gaskell's portrait of "an actual compositor at work": "compositor B of the Shakespeare First Folio" whose own name "may have been John Shakespeare" (348-50): Among B's spelling habits, he preferred "do," "go," and "heere" in contrast with Compositor A's "doe," "goe," and "here." B's work showed "misdirected ingenuity, deliberate tampering, and plain carelessness." In 1619 B set *The Merchant of Venice* using as copy the edition of 1600. If the copy used by B had first been revised by someone else, it has not survived; but "the nature of the alterations" makes it likely that they are B's. Most changes are "clumsy, otiose, or simply wrong." B "quite properly 'rectified' the spelling and punctuation, and used spelling variants for justification" [i.e., to make the lines end evenly at the right margin]. But he also corrected what he thought were "typographical corruptions, mistakes, and even infelicities in the text." His spelling changes were not always consistent: He set "do" 103 times, "doe" 11; "go" 41 times, "goe" 16; "heere" 62 times, "here" 15. He set "doe" only if his copy read "doe"; he set "goe" only once when his copy read "go"; but he set "here" seven times when the copy gave his normal preference "heere." "Thus some of B's spelling preferences were stronger than others." When he used spelling changes for justification of lines, he "plainly preferred" to contract words (260 probable cases) rather than to expand them (96 probable cases). [Perhaps this depended on the particular need of a particular line rather than on what he "plainly preferred".] B made 715 punctuation changes; 347 were added commas.

The reason for some of B's alterations in the text is not clear. For instance at III. i. 40 B's copy read: "I say my daughter is my flesh and my blood"; B omitted the third "my." "Was this because he considered it tautological? because he was trying to make the line into verse (although it is in a prose section)? because he was influenced by the common phrase 'flesh and blood'? or because he left it out accidentally? We cannot tell."

Compositor B made 30 omissions, 16 additions, and 13 transpositions; most of them "seem to have been unintentional mistakes rather than attempts at emendation." Many of B's substitutions (36 of single words, 4 of phrases) "appear to have been mistakes." But B's "major substitution" (I.iii.65-66: "are you resolu'd, How much he would have," instead of "is hee yet possest How much ye would?") was "clearly intentional and was very much in B's style, being an unnecessary solution of a non-existent textual difficulty." B's "largest group of intentional alterations consisted of 27 relatively minor emendations, mostly wrong-headed"—e.g., one "spoiled the verse without improving the sense." The play has 2,648 lines; "B made on average one significant error to every 23 lines."

In a footnote (348) Gaskell cited D. F. McKenzie's "Compositor B's Role in *The Merchant of Venice* Q2 (1619)" in *SB* 12 (1959)75-90; and he then added that "unpublished work by P. W. M. Blayney suggests that *MV* Q2 was set by two compositors, not one." Apparently the allusion was to Blayney's "Compositor B and the Pavier quartos: Problems of Identification and their Implications" (*Library* 5th ser. 27[1972]179-206); here Blayney suggests (203) that *MV* Q2 may have been set by "two supposed compositors" G and H.

So we can say one thing more about Compositor B in the *Merchant of Venice* Q2: he may have been two other guys named G and H.

The compositors of the Shakespeare First Folio have come under the eagle eyes of bibliographers for many years.

In 1932 Willoughby *(Printing of the First Folio*, 55-59), using spelling tests, identified two compositors (A and B) who were at work "during the entire course of the printing" although several plays "show no evidence" of the work of A or B; and he suggested that these and some other plays were set by one or "as is much more likely" two other compositors. But he did not attempt "to make a complete study of the work of the compositors of the Folio, a task belonging rather to the editor of the text than the typographical historian."

In 1953 Hinman identified Compositors A, B, C, D, and that intriguing young man E (in his own day called John Leason) who was an apprentice unable to set properly from manuscript copy and, therefore, employed on printed copy where, alas, he still had his ups and downs. Fredson Bowers traced the Labors of Leason on the Folio *Othello*, using, among other devices, our old friends "do," "go," and "here" (*Bibliography and Textual Criticism* [1964]179-97).

In 1971 Andrew S. Cairncross, using different criteria, redefined the shares of Compositors C and D in setting the Folio (BSA *Papers* 65[1971]41-52). Then in 1972 Cairncross promoted Compositor E from apprentice to experienced (albeit inferior) compositor (not John Leason) and gave him more of the work on the Folio; and he discovered that a brand new Compositor F also had a share in the job (BSA *Papers* 66[1972]369-406). (Blayney had said in a footnote [p. 203] on his naming G and H: "A-E are already in use for Jaggard compositors. I leave F for the possible isolation of a sixth workman in the Folio.")

Perry Mason never had it so tough.

Reappearance of types might be taken to show setting from

presumably the same case by presumably the same compositor; such evidence can perhaps strengthen identification of a compositor by spelling. But it is evidence to be used with great care, cf. Robert K. Turner, Jr.: "Reappearing Types as Bibliographical Evidence" in *SB* 19(1966)198-209. Turner suggested that in one case of "apparent conflict of spelling and typographical evidence" we suppose that "all of Sheet B was set by Compositor A but that B2v and B3 were distributed into [Compositor] B's cases—that is, that the B types were not actually in use by Compositor B until he began work at C3" (202). In another instance "Wilson's workmen did not always maintain control of the same types. We see that although Compositor A set 2L2va, this column was distributed into B's case and that although Compositor B set 2L4a, this column was distributed into A's case" (206).

Fredson Bowers has suggested that sometimes the compositor may be identified by the measure (i.e., page width) of his composing stick (*SB* 2[1949-50]153-167. This, he confesses, is often difficult because often we "must work with variance between two compositor's sticks of as little as a single millimeter" (155). Different compositors seem clearly indicated in his first example where different sets of running titles appear to show simultaneous setting and printing of sections B-F and H-L, and the type page measurements of the two sections are different. But in his next example there are no running titles and the measure in gatherings B-E is 113 mm., F-I 130mm. This may, indeed, mean two different compositors; it may also mean simply that at E the printer decided to make it a shorter book; indeed such an explanation is offered later for similar but more elaborate variations in the measure of Shadwell's *Squire of Alsatia* (1688) (161). In another example (164) the evidence of the measure conflicts with that of spelling tests.

McKenzie wrote that "analysis of a few of the Cambridge books" shows that "not only do the widths of type-pages set by the same compositor vary, but different compositors are often found setting to an identical measure" (23). Finally Moxon remarks that "when several compositors work upon the same book, their measures are all set alike" (41), and it seems possible that so obvious and so practical a rule may have been thought of quite early in the history of printing.

Whodunit? In the years since McKerrow we have come a long way without getting very far. There are at least three problems in the identification of compositors:

1. Available search devices seem to apply largely only to Elizabethan and Jacobean books.
2. Every bibliographer finds his own compositor: Consider the melancholy fate of Compositor B and Compositor E.
3. Is the spelling test really Bibliography? Is it concerned with the book as a *physical object*? Or is it rather concerned with words and sense—i.e., intellectual content?

4. *The Numbers Game*

McKerrow wrote briefly of "Press numbers or working with figures" (81-82). R. W. Chapman had recently called attention to the practice, primarily eighteenth-century, but McKerrow suggested that it was "seldom of much bibliographical importance, as it relates solely to the organization of the printing-house." A small figure "often appears at the foot of a page" (generally a page not bearing a signature) apparently indicating the particular press at which the form containing the figure had been printed. He suggested three possible purposes: (1) "to divide the work equitably" among pressmen, (2) to "serve as a record of the work done by each machine," (3) to be a "check on the pressmen's claims for pay."

Apparently press figures were not always numbers; sometimes they were symbols such as the asterisk. Although a few printers were using press figures when Moxon wrote, there is no reference to them in Moxon's work, nor, indeed, apparently in any eighteenth-century printer's manual. Only with Caleb Stower (1808) do we have explicit mention of the use of press figures. In Chapter XIV ("The Business of an Overseer") Stower urged that the overseer "should be furnished with a book called the press-book" so that "when the pressmen inquire of him what they are to lay on, he informs them, and in this book enters the signature of the sheet, the date when laid on, the number of the press, and the hour" (379). Stower then reproduced a page from such a press-book with separate columns for the various items, and he directed that "before the revise" of the proof of a form "is given to the compositor, the number of the press for which it is intended should be marked in at the bottom of an even page" (381). Finally, under "Rules and Regulations to be observed in a Printing Office," Rule 3 for pressmen reads: "Working without a figure, unless particularly ordered, a fine of three-pence" (386).

John Johnson (1824) repeated the rule (Vol. 2, 489) with footnote: "The custom of working with figures is grown into disuse; in truth they only disfigured the page without being of any utility; the necessity for this is obviated by means of one of the preceding tables." The tables (483 and 485) are similar to the pressbook page reproduced by Stower except that they give pressmen's names instead of press numbers.

Finally, there is the authoritative statement in Savage under "Work with a Figure" (814), the first paragraph apparently written many years before the second:

"In printing offices where there are a number of presses employed, it is usual to distinguish them by numbers . . . and the pressmen put a figure into each form they work, corresponding to the number of their press, for the purpose of ascertaining readily at which press a sheet was printed in case of bad workmanship, or any accident; and in general pressmen are subject to a fine if they work without a figure, or with a wrong one: but when the same press works both the forms of a sheet, it is not necessary to have a figure in more than one form.

The figure used to be placed regularly in a white line at the bottom of an even page . . . it was placed in an even page that it might not mislead the bookbinder; and always in a full page that did not finish a paragraph."

All this seems simple and clear enough. But bibliographers quickly found two problems: (1) Many books of the press figure period have no press figures, and (2) In books containing press figures not all forms are always figured.

Among the first to leap into the fray was Philip Gaskell

(*Library* 5th ser. 4[1949/50]249-261). After a disarming reference to a bibliographer who dubbed his interest in press figures "dehydrated pedantry," he presented a number of tables setting forth the puzzling patterns of press figures in several books. He defended clearly and logically his contention that "sometimes, when one press printed both formes of a sheet, only one of them bore the identifying figure of the press" (252)—a practice described long since by Savage (see above) as Gaskell later discovered himself (*Library* 5th ser. 7[1952]211). Finally he considered how different series of press figures might indicate different impressions of a book.

The most prolific writer on press figures has been William B. Todd. His first major contribution was "Observations on the Incidence and Interpretation of Press Figures" (*SB* 3[1950/51] 171-205). Firmly he announced that "the symbol identifies the man rather than the press" (172, n.3), this in spite of the record of the printers' manuals. Indeed, he felt that "information in the manuals is quite unenlightening" because it is inadequate and because it "indiscriminately reports practices which seemingly vary with the time, the shop, and the number of men employed" (173).

Press figures, he suggested, may often be best interpreted by reference to headlines and skeleton forms. In Gay's *Fables* (1727), a quarto collating A^4 B-Z^4 $2A^2$, for instance, he identified six skeleton forms, "discounting" those for gatherings B, C, and D, which are "indeterminable"; and he presented forms and press figures in the following table (I have *italicized* those forms bearing press figures):

I	E(o) G(o) I(o)	L(i) N(o) P(o)	R(o) T(i) X(i)	*Z(o)*5
II	E(i) G(i) I(i)	*L(o)*5N(i) P(i)	*R(i)*4T(o) *X(o)*4	Z(i)
III	F(o) H(i) K(i)			
IV	F(i) H(o) K(o)			
V		M(o) O(o)	*Q(o)*4S(o) U(o)	*Y(i)*5
VI		*M(i)*7O(i)	Q(i) S(i) U(i)	Y(o)

"The only acceptable interpretation" of the history of the printing he divided into the following sequences:

1. *B-K*: "Two men are . . . assigned to the job at 'half press' (i.e., one man to a machine), their names properly recorded in the ledger." One man (Skeletons I and II) prints both forms of ?C-E-G-I, the other (Skeletons III and IV) both forms of ?B-?D-F-H-K. Then skeletons III and IV are "pied, discarded, or mislaid."

2. *L-P*: Headlines for Skeletons V and VI are composed; "two other men take the place of those originally assigned"; they identify themselves as 5 and 7. Skeletons I and II with pressman 5 print L, N, and P; skeletons V and VI with pressman 7 print M and O.

3. *Q-X*: "Two machines operating . . . at half press" give way to "one machine employing two men (pressman 4 and an assistant) at full press." Q and R bear his figure 4 to show "termination of work by both of his predecessors." Skeletons I and II with pressman 4 print R, T, and X. Skeletons V and VI also with pressman 4 print Q, S, and U. "Unlike the others, 4 anticipates the end of his assignment, and marks it at outer X."

4. *Y-Z*: Skeletons I and II print Z; V and VI print Y. Both accompany pressman 5. Pressman 5 also prints 2A and "presumably *A*."

This suggested history of printing raises several questions:

Press vs. pressman. Would the assumption that the figures indicate (as the printers' manuals suggest) presses instead of men change the suggested history?

Unfigured forms. Why could not the unfigured forms in sequences 2 and 3 (L-X) like those of sequence 1 (B-K) have been done by anonymous pressmen who were content to have "their names properly recorded in the ledger"?

The extra figure. Why did 4 mark the termination of his job at X(o)? No other pressman did this; indeed, it creates confusion if use of a figure can mean *either* the beginning or the end of an assignment.

Pay. If the use of figures established claims to pay or—if payment was not by piecework—credit for good work or blame for poor work, the boss or the pressman would have to reconstruct Todd's table to find out who had done what. A press book such as suggested by the printers' manuals would be far more efficient. Such a book could also tell the number of sheets printed and how long it took. Finally, why fine a man for "working without a figure"? If the printed figure determines his pay, only he would lose by omitting it; his boss would gain.

Skeleton forms and press figures. What is the evidence that a particular press (or pressman) always (or even often) worked only with particular skeleton forms? Such a theory explains Todd's suggested history of the printing of this book, but that does not prove that the theory is correct; for many years a theory that the earth was flat explained many phenomena. What would the pressman (or anyone) gain by such an arrangement? Indeed, such an arrangement would be costly: each skeleton would have to be identified by the printer imposing a form, and this identification would somehow indicate the press to receive that form, and the pressman would somehow know that he (or his press) could (or would) print only certain skeleton forms.

"Two men" and "two other men." How do we *know* that figures 5 and 7 in sequence 2 above are not the same "two men" of sequence 1? Probably the theory is not necessary to the suggested history of the printing.

Time. The vertical lines in Todd's table "indicate the duration of work (possibly a week) for each assignment" (174). This "week" theory led to talk of two men at half press for part of the job and two men at full press for the rest, the phrase "machine only two or three sheets in a week" (with no mention of "possibly"), and finally "work is suspended, over Sunday, we may suppose" (175). The "week" theory, like every time theory in printing, ignores at least two questions: (1) How many copies were printed? (2) How much other work was being done in the shop at the same time? Of course, as with the "two men" theory, probably the "week" theory is not necessary to the suggested history of the printing.

In all of the above Todd assumed that "the symbol identifies the man rather than the press" (172 n.3). But on 176 we find it noted of another book that "a single *press*, first † for A-B, and then * for C-D, seems to be operating." (The italics are mine).

With another book "numbers 2, 3, 4, and occasionally 1 complete the impression of their formes, but † works infrequently

and then only on the press operated by 1. I think we may presume
. . . that 1 is the master printer . . . and has under his tutelage
a young apprentice who is allowed, now and then, to try his
hand. . . . the conjecture follows that where both figures and
symbols appear in the same book, the figures may designate the
master and journeymen, who are assigned numbers according to
seniority, and the symbols, the apprentices, printers' devils, or
'smouters' " (182). We may, indeed, "presume" and if we do
presume it may, indeed, be that "the conjecture follows." But
we face Todd's earlier stern warning about the printers' manuals:
"Thus any theory envisioning a uniform procedure in an unor-
ganized, *laissez-faire* handicraft must be regarded with sus-
picion" (173). It seems not impossible that the warning holds
for bibliographers' presumptions and conjectures no less than
for the printers' precepts.

"The great value of these figures lies in the convenience with
which they may be recorded and subsequently used to distinguish and classify the variants they disclose" (180); this, indeed,
seems to be the major importance of press figures. Todd also
discussed in some detail the use of the figures as corroborative
evidence in establishing the sequence of printing various forms,
the division of copy among several printing houses with differing use of figures, and the like.

Some of Todd's other studies of press figures carried on,
among other things, the theme of distinguishing and classifying
variants. Consider his "Recurrent Printing" (*SB* 12[1959]
189-198). "For many eighteenth-century books the printer sup-
plied only enough copies to meet immediate needs and then,
whenever he could hold the type, reimpressed as often as a
continuing sale might require. . . . Erskine's *View of the
Present War With France* (1797) . . . published 8 A.M. Satur-
day, 11 February, went through nine 'editions' by the end of the
following week, fifteen by the end of the month, twenty-five by
the end of March, and thirty-five shortly thereafter." Todd then
describes twenty titles whose 158 editions "so described by the
printer actually comprise only 28" while most of the other
versions are some form of recurrent impression. Among the
distinguishing features, press figures are frequent.

K. Povey's "A Century of Press Figures" (*Library* 5th ser. 14
[1959]251-273) recorded printer's practice rather than bibliog-

rapher's theory and logic. It reflected his examination of 111 English, Scottish, and Irish octavos of more than five sheets each, printed 1688-1797. To get his 111 he looked at 322 books, including 190 without figures and 21 quartos with figures; 41 percent had figures.

The percentage of books figured rises from about ten in the seventeenth century to about twenty-five in 1701-20 and "in the 1720's it suddenly rises to about 60 and remains fairly constant throughout the rest of the eighteenth century" (253). There are three types: (1) Books with some forms figured, some not (commonest till 1720); (2) Books in which every form is in principle figured even if the same press printed both forms (about 1720 to about 1750); (3) Books with no duplicate figuring of both forms of any sheet. (Type 2 is contrary to Savage's precept noted above.)

"Taking the sample as a whole, 1,132 figures are found on rectos and 1,987 on versos" (254). (This is contrary to Savage's requirement that the figure be on an even page.)

With two books (No. 5, p. 259 and No. 54, p. 260) a press figure did not always accompany the same skeleton form (contrary to the Todd assumption above).

Letters were used as press figures in No. 57 (260), and in footnote 1 Povey tells of letters so used in other books.

There is much variety of practice. "It would be contrary to all experience if Old Ben had not sometimes stood out against the newfangled invention of press figures, or if he had not continued to duplicate his figures after everyone else in the office had given up the practice, or to use them after they had been generally abandoned" (257).

G. Thomas Tanselle's "Press Figures in America: Some Preliminary Observations" (*SB* 19[1966]123-160) is an encyclopedic catalog of details about press figures found "in the course of examining well over a thousand books printed in America between 1775 and 1825" (123). A few of his conclusions may be noted.

Press figures are "quite rare in American books" particularly as compared with "their frequency in English books of the same period," although "certain printers at certain times did use figures extensively and regularly" (123).

There is little evidence to show the meaning of unfigured

forms in otherwise figured books or whether the figures represent men or presses. He did, however, suggest that "there does not seem to be a great deal of point in indicating . . . the number of the press . . . except as a record of the work done by a particular man at that press" (127, n. 13); in short, the figure represents *both* man and press—regardless of its user's intent. [Perhaps there were two kinds of "record of the work," each serving its own purpose: (1) The figure printed in the form would at once betray the press (and perhaps thereby the pressman) responsible for an error, and (2) the entry in the press book of Stower and Johnson would at once justify payment to the pressman.]

For two volumes he suggested that "the unfigured formes clearly represent work by another pressman, since the usual pattern is for each sheet to consist of one figured and one unfigured forme" (129)—although this "usual pattern" is precisely what would be the result of Savage's precept: "When the same press works both the forms of a sheet, it is not necessary to have a figure in more than one form."

Occasionally figures occur on the signature page (130 and 131).

Tanselle's "two most extensive examples" discovered were "in Philadelphia by several printers (especially Thomas Dobson) in the 1790's and . . . in New York by Isaac Riley and Charles Wiley in the 1810's." Dobson, using four figures, "figured about 66% of the quarto formes . . . for his *Encyclopaedia*, figured 36% of the sheets in both formes, and figured 85% of the outer formes. . . . Riley, using six figures, figured 73% of the formes in his legal octavos in half sheet, Wiley 93%" (157).

Keith I. D. Maslen's " 'Press' Letters: Samuel Aris 1730-32" (*SB* 23[1970]119-126) told of a "few letters, upper or lower case, placed one in each forme or sheet with occasional omissions" at the foot of certain pages in London books printed by Samuel Aris 1730-32 (see also above, p. 63). Apparently they serve as press figures. One book uses C, J, R, and W; another uses C, F, I, J, R, T, and W. Because it is unlikely that Aris would have had as many presses as there are letters used, Maslen suggested that "it is intrinsically probable" that the letters "refer to men, perhaps by the initial of their surname" (120-121). Just as Todd and others had shown with press figures, so Maslen showed that press letters also can often distinguish between "reissue, reimpression, and divided printing" (121).

Elsewhere Maslen noted that in the printing of the *Votes of the House of Commons,* 1730-1781, press figures "do not consistently tally with the press-record, chiefly because of an evident failure to figure some formes" (*Library* 5th ser. 25[1970]123).

J. D. Fleeman's "William Somerville's *The Chace,* 1735" (BSA *Papers* 58[1964]1-7) traced the history of the printing of *The Chace* as set forth in the ledger of its printer, William Bowyer and compared it with the book itself. The ledger records the work of compositors and of press men. For press work, the name of the book and the number of copies printed is followed by entries for forms in vertical columns, one column for each press headed by its number and the names of the pressmen who work it. Apparently here the press figure stood for both press and men. There are columns for presses numbered 1, 2, 3, and 8. For five forms the press figure indicated by the ledger differs from that printed in the form (4-5). There were two skeleton forms and they "were passed from press to press as required, so that there can be no supposing that each press had its own skeletons by which it can be identified" (6); cf. Todd above. The ledger also records work on other books being printed in Bowyer's shop at the same time as *The Chace*: The first entry for *The Chace* is under April 5, 1735, recording type set for B; the last entry is under May 24, recording press work on A. "It is important . . . that any interpretation of press figures should be undertaken with the utmost care"; in the case of *The Chace* "without the benefit of the printing records . . . a good many serious misinterpretations would have been the result of the usual kinds of analysis" (7).

Finally, consider the Cambridge University pressman, John Terrill (McKenzie 50-51). Terrill came up from London in late November 1701 and he left Cambridge again May 15, 1703. Cambridge pressmen at that time "did not normally use press figures," but Terrill did. His "bills for presswork match the figures exactly and make it perfectly clear that, in this case, the figures represent a man . . . not a press. Terrill did not always use a figure, nor keep to the same one; and it is certain that here in the Cambridge house his use of a figure was a purely personal and optional matter. His main reason for using one at all would seem to have been that the first two volumes of *Suidas* were being printed concurrently" with some chance of confusing the signatures of one volume for those of another. "So Terrill played safe by marking the sheets that he printed," although his figure appears only in one form of each sheet. His "main concern seems to have been merely to use some idiosyncratic mark, and once the work had been paid for, any other might serve as well"; thus he used at different times two different figures (* and ‡) in both volumes.

So, if the tumult and the shouting should die, what is left? Not much really.

1. Press figures occur in many books printed between about 1680 and about 1820.

2. Probably they refer to the press, not the pressman; but a particular press seems often to have meant also the particular pressman or press crew who worked it.

3. Probably they do not represent claims for pay; the written record of work which printers' manuals recommend would do that far better and much more quickly. Perhaps they did offer a quick way to determine responsibility for any mistake.

4. Use of press figures was quite irregular; many books have none and many have only some here and there. Apparently some shops required them and fined pressmen for forgetting to use them; apparently some shops did not require them. Men may have moved from a figure shop to a non-figure shop and carried the practice with them like McKenzie's John Terrill. Or men may simply have grown old in the job like Povey's "Old Ben" and stuck to the old ways, whatever they were.

5. If used with caution, press figures can sometimes help bibliographers (a) as supplementary evidence of some bit of printing history established by other means, and/or (b) as points of distinction between different impressions.

The Numbers Game is quite a game; but you may not win much at it.

5. *Of Pots and Crowns and Grapes and Such*

We begin with McKerrow: "A knowledge of the processes by which paper is manufactured and of the substances of which it is composed has never, I think, been regarded as necessary to the bibliographer, however important it may be to the librarian and it is no part of my intention to deal with such matters here. . . . It would undoubtedly be of use to us in the solution of many bibliographical problems if we had more exact knowledge . . . of paper . . . but much detailed work will be necessary before any connected view of the subject becomes available." He the offered a few "desultory notes" on such matters as history, manufacture, watermarks, and sizes of hand-made paper (97-108). Since McKerrow, bibliographers have done "much detailed work" on these and other aspects of paper.

Paper is, of course, important in the study of bibliography because the basic unit of the book as a physical object is a gathering of leaves, each gathering produced by folding a part of a large sheet of paper, a whole sheet, or several sheets. For many centuries all paper was made by hand. Linen rags were beaten to a pulp and stirred with water. Workmen dipped out the mixture in shallow trays or "molds" with wire bottoms and removable wooden sides called "deckles." As the water drained away, the pulp settled in a thin layer on the wire bottom and the mold was shaken in such a way that the fibers interlocked. The edges of the paper were rough and uneven where the pulp had come against the deckles. The wire bottom of the mold impressed a design on the sheet. A number of heavy lines run across the sheet; these are called "chain lines." At right angles to these chain lines are many other lines, fainter and much closer together; these are called "wire lines." Generally there is also a "watermark," a device or symbol (e.g., a pot or a crown or a bunch of grapes) located at or near the middle of one-half of the sheet. In some paper there is also a "countermark" located at or near the middle of the other half of the sheet. By the end of the eighteenth century "wove" paper was rather common. The molds for such paper had bottoms of closely woven wire and for that reason the paper shows traces of neither chain lines nor wire lines; the woven wire principle was carried into the machine-made paper of the nineteenth century.

Among the more prolific writers about paper was Allan Stevenson. One of his early studies drew largely on an examination of watermarks in several copies of each title in a group of play quartos printed by Thomas Cotes in spring 1639/40: "New Uses of Watermarks as Bibliographical Evidence" (*SB* 1[1948-9]151-182). Watermarks of paper in Shirley's *Opportunitie* and *Coronation* included a pot, the Christian symbol IHS with cross on the bar of the H, a bird, and grapes; Stevenson noted that they appear in gatherings as indicated in the following table:

Opportunitie A² B-K⁴		*Coronation* A² B-I⁴ K²	
A	Grapes	A	Grapes
B-F	Pot, IHS, Bird	B-E	Bird, Grapes, Belt, IHS
G-K	Grapes almost completely	F-K	Grapes almost completely

"The inference is inescapable: *The Coronation* was going through the press at very nearly the same time as *The Opportunitie.* . . . The simplest explanation is that the two plays were being printed on separate presses fed by the same job-lot supply of paper" (163). "Everyone knows that in first editions the preliminaries were commonly printed last, but everyone cannot readily demonstrate the fact"; in this case, however, the table shows that "A of both these plays was printed at least among the last" (179).

With regard to his discovery that the watermarks in two copies of a play by William Habington differ throughout: "My guess is that Habington, a butterfly sort of courtier poet, had a number of copies printed on better-grade paper for himself and his friends, and that Tom Cotes simply included a token or so of this paper in the paper laid out for each sheet" (181).

Stevenson combined his *Opportunitie* watermarks with skeleton forms, press corrections, written records, and other evidence; the result is mighty smooth: "After some three years in Ireland, Shirley returned to England in mid-April 1640. He must have reached London about Monday, April 20. As he found his play, 'emergent from the Presse and prepar'd to seeke entertainment abroad,' we may take it that sheets B to K were then printed and ready, or sheet K was coming from the press. Reckoning back in terms of 1500 copies, a single press, and the skeleton shifts, we can make a schedule with tentative dates. It starts on April Fool's day and need not be taken as revelation" (177).

In this passage Stevenson chose April 20 because "a week later, on April 28, two plays which he probably had brought with him from Ireland were entered on the Register by Richard Whitaker" (footnote 73). The "1500 copies" goes back to p. 158-159: "The edition was probably one of 1500 copies. This quantity best satisfies both the distribution ratios [of watermarks and press corrections] and the external evidence. If we adopt the working assumption that each watermark . . . represents a half-token of paper . . . we can follow the course of the press (or presses) from paper to paper fairly well. . . ." Footnote 23 remarked that "A case might be made for 2000 copies. . . ." Finally: "We may suppose that Cotes's well-ordered establishment, using two skeletons, normally printed and perfected about 1000 sheets (two reams) on one press in one day. Thus, in machining an edition of 1500, completion of a sheet would tend to coincide with the end of the work-day every third day. . . . if all went well the presswork on four edition sheets might neatly fill a week" (166).

"Probably . . . probably . . . assumption . . . fairly well . . . suppose . . . normally . . . tend . . . if all went well . . . might neatly fill . . ." and an assumed "well-ordered establishment."

In any event, we have a "schedule with tentative dates" accounting for every day April 1 through April 22 (177-178). Included are such details as "A compositor would set about six pages on the first day, and printing might begin on the morning of the 2d" and "The late corrections in inner C may be due to the late arrival of the Cotes brothers or their corrector on Easter Monday".

And so, "Though there is no way to check the details of this schedule, the general idea in it seems right enough . . . and through analogy we can measure the amount of time Cotes took to print *The Coronation*, and perhaps the whole series of 1639/40 Fletcher-Shirley Quartos" (178). All this by combining watermarks with skeleton forms and by building "probably" into "we can measure."

With "Watermarks are Twins" (*SB* 4[1951-52]57-91) Stevenson moved to firmer ground. He noted that the "moderate mixture of papers generally found in books" is only the natural result of packing in quires and reams and bales, transportation, and storage in the warehouse or on the printer's shelves. In all of this the paper "had been sorted rather according to size and quality than according to make and mark" (59-60).

But even before that a difference had been introduced: Regularly the vatman used two similar molds. After he had dipped up pulp on one mold he removed the deckle and passed on the mold and its sheet to his helper, who allowed the sheet to dry a bit and then turned it out onto felt. Meanwhile the vatman had picked up another mold, placed the deckle about it, and was dipping again.

Twin molds, Stevenson noted, mean twin watermarks. "It was enough if a pair of moulds resembled each other so closely that the vatman would always know them for mates" (64), but Stevenson listed ten points of possible differences between the twins such as marks placed in different halfsheets ("some marks read *in* and some read *out*"), marks with different relation to nearby chainlines, marks slanting differently, different labels (e.g., one mark with full name, the other with only initials), different countermarks, different position of "dots" (made by the sewing-wire attaching the mark), different distortions because of deterioration.

So differing watermarks may not mean different paper: "The basic equation is: Two watermarks equal one paper" (89).

In "Paper as Bibliographical Evidence" (*Library* 5th ser. 17 [1962]197-212) Stevenson stated in some detail his method of study. Previous work by others had been based on tracings of watermarks, chiefly taken from manuscripts. This, he felt, was enough for dealing with types of watermarks, "but unless we can be *sure* of the identity of two marks . . . we have little chance of solving, convincingly, through paper evidence, such a problem as the date of an incunable" (199). He proposed precise measurements and careful photography. Each mold is "likely to have produced a half million sheets in its lifetime" (199), and if the bibliographer examines many leaves of books identical marks from particular molds will turn up. His method involved "Runs, States, and Sewing Dots":

Runs: Scribes or notaries might use a supply of paper with the same watermark over a long period of time; but printers tended to use up a supply of paper on a book before going to the next batch. So "we often find *runs* of a single paper for many gatherings" in a book before the printer "proceeds to runs of other papers, usually papers of similar quality" (201-202). From printers' records it seemed clear to Stevenson that paper was bought for the printing of a particular book and probably not long after that paper's manufacture. It is true that a random watermark dated (say) 1598 can turn up in a gathering in a book dated 1605; but this probably comes from sheets of stock left over from an earlier book. So Stevenson had his Principle of Runs and Remnants: "*Running paper* is relevant to the dating of a book; *random paper* is unreliable for the purpose" (202).

States: "Ordinarily a much-used pair of moulds lasts but a year or two; and the wires that impress the watermarks deteriorate in a shorter time" (203). The mark changes both in exact shape and in exact location, so that the various states of a watermark betray its aging and the bibliographer can sometimes trace these states from book to book or even within the same book.

Sewing Dots: An early watermark form might be sewed to its mold at 20 points; and the position of the resulting sewing dots impressed in the paper differs even between twins, and might often remain even if the watermark wires moved from one state to another.

The second part of this article dealt with application of the method and drew on work described in detail in Stevenson's fascinating book *The Problem of the Missale Speciale* (1967).

The *Missale Speciale* has been assigned dates ranging from 1445 to 1490 (167), largely on the basis of study of the type. In *The Problem* Stevenson worked chiefly with the watermarks of the book. There are three pairs of them: a bull's head with a tau between the horns, a tall cross on three mounts, and another bull's head with tau. He examined every leaf of the four known copies of the *Missale,* and after long search he discovered eleven other books, all of the 1470s, which contained paper made from the same molds as that of the *Missale.* By study of the variant states of their watermarks as they deteriorated, he was able to arrange these states, and thus the books in which they appeared, in a rough time sequence. The fact that three pairs of marks "proceed from fresh youth to decrepit age, within the leaves of the Missal and the associated books . . . must quiet misgivings and fears" (155-56). The evidence seems to show that the *Missale Speciale* was printed during 1473.

As with Shirley's *Opportunitie*, Stevenson then tried to set up a definite work schedule, "assuming a minimum rate of progress and a maximum work period," and drawing on evidence outside the book. His schedule runs from February through October, but he admitted that "because of the number of hypotheses and assumptions" and the fact that "we do not know how fast an early printer might set and print" the result is "highly conjectural" (166-167).

Curt F. Bühler's "Last Words on Watermarks" (BSA *Papers* 67[1973]1-16), while accepting Stevenson's date for the *Missale Speciale*, insisted on skepticism in using paper for dating. He pointed out that paper molds had a limited life only if they were used continuously, that all the paper produced by a mold was not always used up in two or three years, that paper was not used by the printer in the same order in which it came from the mold, and that some dealers did now and then accumulate stocks of paper. Stevenson had remarked that the "consensus" is that a pair of molds lasted a year "when in continuous use" (*Problem* 316); and at James Whatman's the average life of a pair of molds was "just over seven months" (Gaskell 63, n. 12).

A famous book containing a great variety of watermarks is the collection of Shakespeare plays in quarto bearing different individual dates but actually all printed in 1619 as shown by typographical evidence. In this volume Stevenson found a watermark dated 1608 in a play dated 1600 and a watermark with date 1617 or 1619 in a play dated 1608 (*SB* 4[1951-52]159-64 and Greg, Vol. 3, p. 1107).

Pots and Crowns and Grapes and Such can lead us far, but they are tricky guides.

6. *Something Old and Something New*

We begin with McKerrow: "To the bibliographer the decorations of books are as a rule of much more importance than the illustrations on account of the greater amount of information which he can derive from them. . . . the blocks were often used again and again for long periods, even sometimes for a hundred years or more. This fact may be very useful in helping us to trace the printers of books which bear no printer's name and to ascertain the date of printing of undated books, for on the one hand we may possess good evidence as to the ownership of the block at the particular time, and on the other, as the block gradually deteriorated by use we may be able to place the particular impression between two others the dates of which are known to us . . . Decorations may be roughly divided into ornaments, ornamental initials, printers' and other devices, and woodcut borders . . . " (113-114). Elsewhere he suggested that such evidence may also help identify portions of a book printed at a house different from that named in the imprint (128-129). As an aid in the use of decorations, McKerrow prepared illustrated lists such as his *Printers' and Publishers' Devices in England and Scotland* (1913).

Identification of unnamed printers, dating of undated books, preparing illustrated lists of ornamental decorations: bibliographers have continued to move steadily ahead in all three areas.

Willoughby, for instance, suggested (*Printing of the First Folio* [1932]36) that those portions of the Shakespeare First Folio and those portions of another book containing a particular tailpiece with only one defect were printed before the later pages of a third book containing this same tailpiece with a second defect—even though the third book was published before the other two. An ornament in the undated first edition of Richard Hooker's *Ecclesiastical Polity* is slightly damaged when it appears in a book printed early in 1594; Hooker's book may thus have been printed in 1593 (BSA *Papers* 41[1947]345). Similar evidence indicates that the *Iliads* in one issue of *The Whole Works of Homer* (1616?) were reprinted in 1633 or 1634 (BSA *Papers* 40[1946]231). William B. Todd showed that the undated so-called counterfeit of an Aldine Cicero (*Le Pistole ad Attico*) contains Aldine ornamental initials and a genuine Aldine anchor device whose condition places the printing of the book btween an Aldine book printed in 1556 and another printed in 1557. In the course of the study he noted also that two other books dated 1558 "were printed concurrently, as each contains leaves with the anchor first in original state, then in later condition" (BSA *Papers* 60[1966]413-417). Such use of printers' device deterioration may be compared with Stevenson's use of watermark deterioration (see above p. 71-72).

Just as Todd was able to prove that a counterfeit was genuine, so W. A. Jackson showed that a genuine was counterfeit. In 1613 Thomas Creede printed an edition of Wither's *Abuses Stript and Whipt* using close copies of George Eld's initials and ornaments with even the cracks and other defects reproduced (*Library* 4th ser. 15[1935]364-376).

Elsewhere Jackson told of a non-bibliographer historian who spent some time tracing the wandering of Bishop Aylmer in 1559 because a book by Aylmer of that date named Strassburg in its imprint; actually, the initials and ornaments show that the book was printed in London by John Day (2).

On the basis of ornaments and pictorial initials, Colin Clair was able to show that a number of English Reformation tracts with fictitious imprints were actually printed by Steven Mierdman, some on the continent and some in London. Ironically, when the accession of Mary Tudor forced Mierdman to leave England in 1553, much of his material passed to Richard Jugge and John Cawood, the latter appointed royal printer in 1553 (*Library* 5th ser. 18[1963]275-287).

Bradford F. Swan told of a print shop receiving in spring 1637 a closely sealed packet containing a "brand new letter" C carved in boxwood for use in printing one of William Prynne's tracts. The letter served a two-fold purpose: (1) Because it was new it was "unknown among the printers of London," and (2) "Turned in one direction, it revealed a pope's head, and, turned the other way, it showed 'an army of men and soldiers' " (*Gregory Dexter of London and New England* [1949]11). Initials and ornaments enabled Swan to identify a number of books connected with Dexter. Similarly Mark H. Curtis was able to show that a number of Puritan tracts of 1604 to 1609 were printed (not by Richard Schilders or other continental printers but) probably by Richard Jones in London (*Library* 5th ser. 19[1964]38-66).

By study of ornaments and initials, J. A. Lavin was able to add nineteen titles to the thirty-eight already known to have been printed by the Elizabethan printer, John Danter—an increase of fifty percent (*SB* 23[1970]39). With ornaments and initials, Lavin was also able to identify the various printers of seven Jonson quartos (*Library* 5th ser. 25[1970]331-338). Elsewhere Lavin traced some of the use during 1590-1640 of three ornamental blocks of similar design all showing, among other features, an owl "wearing a round flat hat with four tassels" and apparently originally cut "for some specific anti-papist work." Among other things this study showed that (1) it takes more than a spot check to show that a printer did not own a particular ornament; one of the owls appeared in only 4 of 139 books printed by W. Stansby, and (2) the passing of blocks from one printer to another can help in the study of the printers' careers (*Library* 5th ser. 22 [1967]143-147).

Ornaments and initials have also helped identify printers not named in the imprint of a book who nonetheless printed a portion or portions of the book. R. C. Bald, for instance, was able to show that various sections of the Beaumont and Fletcher First Folio were printed by Thomas Warren, William Wilson, Ruth Raworth, Edward Griffin, and Robert White (*Bibliographical Studies in the Beaumont & Fletcher Folio of 1647* [1938]13-19). Ornamental initials show that the second half of the 1602 pamphlet *Work for Chimny-Sweepers* was printed by Thomas Creede although the imprint names only T. Este as printer (BSA *Papers* 42[1948]149). P. W. M. Blayney found that nearly a third of the over seventy books on which the Snowden/Okes house worked during 1606-1609 were shared (BSA *Papers* 67[1973] 437-442). Examples are frequent in Greg—e.g., I, no. 202(a) and (b) and III, 1016, 1058, and 1117. William A. Jackson predicted that "hundreds and even thousands of anonymously printed books will, in the revision of the *Short-Title Catalogue*, have been ascribed to particular printers" (11); and Katharine F. Pantzer wrote on intentions in the revised STC to "indicate what portions of a text are the work of each printer where two or more are involved" (BSA *Papers* 62[1968]304).

A great help in identification is the illustrated list of type ornaments, and ornamental initials. C. William Miller, for instance, produced such illustrated lists of Benjamin Franklin's

Philadelphia type (*SB* 11[1958]179-206) and of the Restoration printer Thomas Newcomb's ornament stock (*SB* 3[1950/51] 155-170). Perhaps Miller's most ambitious and most interesting study was "A London Ornament Stock: 1598-1683" (*SB* 7[1955] 125-151). Carefully he traced the general line of succession of the printers involved from Thomas Judson through Margaret White with the facts of their careers and the terminal dates of each man's use of the stock. He was quite aware of the pitfalls: "They could always purchase new decorations or acquire them at second hand. . . . they lent blocks which they never saw again, or borrowed others which they neglected to return; they . . . commissioned imitations or recuttings of decorations which caught their fancy. . . . with reluctance did they discard permanently. . . . decorations which fell into disuse were shoved back . . . rather than thrown away. . . . the 'pear' A that flourished . . . before the defeat of the Spanish Armada . . . reappeared in print finally in the year of the Restoration" (125). But such a list has great value—e.g., the printers who used these blocks during the last fifty years left many of their imprints unsigned; but they printed "a good portion of the significant belles lettres in mid-seventeenth-century London" (135).

Among other lists we may note H. R. Hoppe's work on John Wolfe (*Library* 4th ser. 14[1933]241-288, J. A. Lavin's list of John Danter's ornaments (*SB* 23[1970]21-44), and K. I. D. Maslen *The Bowyer Ornament Stock* (1973).

So much for labor in the old-time vineyard. Workers also moved into a new field.

"Far too often in recent bibliographical studies, particularly those using the newer techniques of type-shortages, compositor identification, printing order of formes, etc., one reads phrases in which the words 'likelihood,' 'probable,' 'apparent,' etc., recur with alarming frequency. These papers have been prepared with vast labor—one is sometimes informed of the exact number of pieces of type, which on a given day were in a particular box of of the compositor's case—and one can well imagine innumerable manuscript tables which were prepared to confirm the more striking examples which are printed. We seem to be looking over the compositor's shoulder, watching his every movement, or assisting the pressman as he turns his piles of paper to begin perfecting them. But do we really know so much? Did our compositor suffer that day from a surfeit of beer? Did the pressman really have his mind on what he was doing and was he not thinking of his domestic troubles? They were not automatic machines,—and even if they were, the number of times the machine which packages my cigarettes put the ribbon inside the wrapper instead of outside would give one reason to be wary" (Jackson 13).

Well, what really did happen in the print shop? Has the bibliographer's zeal for study of the book as a physical object caused him to ignore evidence outside the physical book? Has logic based on what he seemed to have found in the physical object caused him even to ignore common sense? Must the evidence of the physical book itself conform with outside evidence? Will it be true bibliography if it goes beyond the evidence of the physical book itself?

What is this outside evidence?

First of all, of course, there have long been the printers' manuals. Moxon, it is true, is scarce; and the De Vinne reprint of 1896 had itself become a rare book. All this changed with the scholarly edition by Herbert Davis and Harry Carter (1958, 2d ed., 1962). Hard on its heels came the Gregg English Bibliographical Sources [Reproductions] ed. by D. F. Foxon, Ser. 3: Printers' Manuals—James Watson (1713), John Smith (1755), Philip Luckombe (1771), Caleb Stower (1808), John Johnson (1824), Thomas C. Hansard (1825), Charles H. Timperley (1838), and William Savage (1841). Now the bibliographer can work— if he will—with the whole array of English printers' manuals at his elbow. True, he can complain that Moxon goes back only to 1683. But E. C. Bigmore and C. W. H. Wyman (*Bibliography of Printing*, 1884), Lawrence C. Wroth (*Typographic Heritage* [1949]55-90), H. Davis (*Printing and Graphic Arts* 5[1957]17-33), and Davis and Carter's Appendix VII all confirm what some of the authors of manuals since Moxon have themselves now and then admitted: Each goes back to Moxon in greater or less extent and sometimes even uses his phrases. Can we believe that a craft which has been so traditional since Moxon was not traditional also before Moxon? The brief accounts of printing written before Moxon seem in general to agree with Moxon; cf. D. C. Allen, "Some Contemporary Accounts of Renaissance Printing Methods" (*Library* 4th ser. 17[1937]167-170) and the dialogue attributed to Plantin edited with translation by Ray Nash in *Calligraphy & Printing in the Sixteenth Century* (1964).

This is not to suggest that the manuals are a detailed statement of universal practice. Printers were as they are (and as Jackson suggests) only men. They had their good days and their bad days, their dislikes and their preferences, their training and their neglect of training. For example, the difference between the manuals' words on press figures and the printers' use of press figures is notorious. This is not too surprising; among bibliographers even the most devout disciple of Fredson Bowers departs now and then from his precepts.

Moreover, the manuals themselves are sometimes confusing. For instance, Moxon's somewhat tangled remarks on "hours" and "tokens" (344 and elsewhere) have long seemed to answer the bibliographer's yearning for a flat statement of a never varying speed of all presswork, although Savage (323) makes it clear that the pressman's "hour" always equals a token but not always only sixty minutes; see also Davis and Carter (2d ed., 484-486): "It must have varied with the size of the sheet, the format, and the density of the setting, among other things; so that statistics, if they are available, would need interpretation."

Some more modern books helped rescue the printer from the bibliographer's world of logic and fancy. Ellic Howe's *The London Compositor* (1947) and "*The Trade*": *Passages from the Literature of the Printing Craft, 1550-1935* (1943) confronted the bibliographer with documents relating to everyday life in the print shop, wages, working conditions, and customs. The vivid autobiography of Charles Manby Smith, *The Working Man's Way in the World* (1857, Reprinted 1967), told how it really was with a compositor in mid-nineteenth-century England. Also there were biographies such as Helmut Lehmann-Haupt's *Peter Schoeffer* (1950), Colin Clair's *Christopher Plantin* (1960), and Elizabeth Armstrong's *Robert Estienne* (1954). The American scene appeared in books such as Lawrence C. Wroth's *Colonial Printer* (1938) and Rollo G. Silver's *The American Printer 1787-1825* (1967).

Perhaps most helpful of all have been the printers' own records. William Strahan's ledgers, for instance, found and placed in the British Museum in 1956, tell much of what was "normal" in a major English printing house from 1738 to 1785. Patricia Hernlund (*SB* 20[1967]89-111) is concerned primarily with Strahan's bookkeeping methods and charging patterns; but she also makes clear such things as the major role of job work "as a practical way to 'fill unsold time' " between book work (95); and the fact that "the unit charge was always based on type, the size of the sheet, and the number of copies run" (106). Money charged means time spent; obviously the bibliographer must consider these factors along with the logic of a book as a physical object when he comes to suggest how long (and why) it took to print that particular book. We have seen above (p. 65-66) how study of the Bowyer-Nichols ledgers and the Cambridge University press records deals with press figure mythology. The Cambridge primary records are in volume II of D. F. McKenzie's *Cambridge University Press 1696-1712* (1966), and K. I. D. Maslen is editing the Bowyer records for publication by the Bibliographical Society.

The Prophet of the New Incredulity is D. F. McKenzie, and his warning rings loud and clear: "Printers of the Mind: Some Notes on Bibliographical Theories and Printing-House Practices" (*SB* 22[1969]1-75). He is literate, logical, philosophical, and his array of facts are pitiless. He drew on the Cambridge Press records with material also from the Bowyer and other records. These records reveal in detail the week-by-week operations of a printing house and make it easy to draw up "detailed production charts for the books printed, showing their progress sheet by sheet, and recording the exact division of work between different compositors, correctors and pressmen." They make it simple also "to offer definitive details on the wages earned, and the actual amount of work done by compositors and press-crews and to construct work-flow diagrams. . . . The patterns which emerge seem to me to be of such an unpredictable complexity, even for such a small printing shop, that no amount of inference from what we think of as bibliographical evidence could ever have led to their reconstruction" (7). A number of McKenzie's facts and/or conclusions are listed briefly below;

1. *Workmen's Output* (8-12).

"Wages, and therefore output, since the men were on piece-rates, varied considerably as between one man and another" and "any one man's . . . output might fluctuate greatly week by week" (8). At Cambridge "the only compositor to show sustained application at a high level was Thomas Pokins" and his "averages throughout 1702 were 6,307 (not 10,000 or 12,000) ens a day" (9). ["10,000 or 12,000" had been the product of the bibliographer's logic.] As to press work: From mid-June to mid-July 1700 Robert Ponder and John Quinny had a weekly production rate of impressions ranging from 9,700 to 17,000 (10). [The "hypothetical norm" set by the bibliographer had been 18,000.] Moxon remarks (327) that journeymen "are by contract with the master printer paid proportionably *for what they undertake to earn* every working day, be it half a crown, two shillings, three shillings, &"; and we note that Moxon here "speaks quite casually of a performance difference of one hundred percent" (11). Thus a man worked only to meet his individual contract, and he was penalized only if he fell behind his contracted figure and kept a colleague waiting. We have, then, the "normality of non-uniformity . . . uncomfortable . . . for any methodology" (12).

2. *Edition Size* (13-14).

Bibliographers have tended to think in terms of the 1250-1500 copies set by the Stationers' company ordinance of 1587 although McKerrow had warned (132) that we do not know how long or how well this rule was followed. Variability in edition size creates problems; "even in the early 1590s a pressman, Simon Stafford, giving evidence in court, pointed out that the number of sheets printed in any one day might vary considerably, reflecting different edition sizes" (13). The Cambridge records show editions ranging from 350 to 3,000, and other printers' records show similar variation (14). So work organization in the print shop had to deal with this variable as well as with the varying output of the men.

3. *Concurrent production* (14-22).

"It is the assumption that even if the whole resources of a house were not directed towards printing the book under examination, at least one compositor and one press-crew would be set to work fairly consistently on it. Under these conditions we might expect five to six sheets a week to be completed." But at Cambridge "out of some 36 books of ten or more sheets produced between 1698 and 1705, only 7 were printed at an average rate of more than 2 sheets a week." Moreover, "evidence from the Bowyer and Ackers ledgers points exactly the same way" (14-15). Obviously these houses "habitually printed several books concurrently. So far as I am aware there is no primary evidence whatever to show that any printing house of the 16th, 17th or 18th centuries did not do likewise." This allowed greater flexibility in the efficient organization of the shop's *total* production even though work on individual books moved more slowly than the bibliographer's logic might lead us to expect (16). McKerrow had suggested that in an efficient shop there would be "a definite correspondence between rate of composition and the output of the machine room" and bibliographers assumed that this meant work on an individual book (17). Yet "of the 13 compositors whose work for Bowyer over a two-week period early in 1732 is recorded . . . only *one* was engaged on one book alone" (18); and at Cambridge between 26 Dec. 1701 and 28 Feb. 1702 "the various sheets of any particular book were likely as not printed at more than one press" (21-22). So, although we may assume "that composition and presswork *as a whole* were fairly economically balanced, it would be quite wrong to conclude that this balance was either necessary or possible for work on any individual book" (22).

    4. *Compositors' Measures* (22-23).

"If we assume concurrent production . . . then the likelihood of measures reflecting the division of work among compositors will be small" because (1) "production times were too long" and (2) "compositors working on several books at a time . . . would have to change their measure constantly" (23). The Cambridge evidence bears out these suggestions (see above p. 56).

    5. *Skeleton Forms* (23-36).

Much speculation about skeleton forms rests on the assumption underlying a statement by Bowers in 1942: If a single skeleton was used for both forms of a sheet, "the press was idle while the forme just off the press was being washed and stripped and its skeleton . . . transferred to the type pages . . . next to be printed. . . . Some printers used two skeletons. . . . Thus while one forme was on the press" the other was being "imposed about the type pages next to be printed. . . . there was no delay at all" (24).

"The press was idle." Efficiency demanded two skeletons for one press—if composition and press work are in balance. In a small edition, composition would lag behind press work and there would be no need of a second skeleton; with a large edition, the reverse would be true (Hinman). And so Bowers feels that "certain assumptions can be made about the rate of compositorial to press speed and thus about the number of copies printed" (25). Also with two skeletons it is possible to correct one form while the other is being printed (26).

If efficiency generally requires two skeleton forms for one press, do two skeleton forms in a book mean there was one press? Greg and Bowers were somewhat skeptical about using skeleton forms as evidence of presses, but bibliographers have done just that to prove the existence of one press, two presses (Bowers himself did this), "at least two presses," and "at least four presses." Moreover, some write of "a normal pattern for two-compositor work in which each man serves a different press" (27), while another states that "one skeleton ordinarily means one compositor" (28).

"The press was idle"; with concurrent production this would not be the result. This section concluded with an account of the skeleton forms and ledgers for three Cambridge books. The first is Beaumont's *Psyche* (1702) gatherings 2E-2Z "which can be related to full work-flow charts." The edition was 750; two compositors set it, but only one worked on it at a time; four skeleton forms were in regular use; printing was at more than one press, sometimes full press, sometimes half press; and setting and printing of these 38 sheets lasted from mid-September 1701 to 31 Jan. 1702. "And yet if this evidence were not available it would be perfectly respectable to infer that this regular use of four skeletons might mean (a) a large edition; or (b) two compositors if not three; or (c) at least one full press in continuous operation" (29-30).

    6. *Casting Off Copy* (37-42).

"Neither the Cambridge nor Bowyer records offer much posi-

tive evidence of setting by formes; although their combined testimony does demonstrate the rarity of such a practice for books
other than page-for-page reprints and must therefore give us
pause. . . . The most important reason for setting by formes in
quarto is unlikely to have been urgency, nor even an unusually
small fount, but a fount *depleted* because of concurrent printing
—for if work overlapped on two or more books using the same
fount . . . setting by formes would offer a method of making
some progress with all" (40).

    7. *Proof Correction* (42-49).

    Although Moxon gave very detailed instructions for proof
correction, Bowers rejected the Moxon procedure for Elizabethan
and Jacobean printing because it would have "interrupted the
printing whenever a forme to be proofed was prepared" (43); and
Hinman rejected it because "there are far too many obvious
errors of all kinds in far too many Folio pages" if the Moxon
procedure had been followed (43). But "one might ask whether
it is likely that the essentially trivial corrections noted by Professor Hinman would have been made at all if the printer were
indifferent to the accuracy of his text" because they involved "so
many bibliographically serious delays at press" (46). Moreover,
"the '*Proofe*, and *Reuiewes*' pulled by Jaggard [the Folio Printer]
for Brooke's *Catalogue* testify to the currency of Moxon's terms
at this time, and in Jaggard's shop (McKerrow, 207)" (46).
Ashley's translation of Louis Le Roy, *Of the Interchangeable
Course* (1594) contains a passage on proofing which agrees with
Moxon; although Hinman discounts the testimony "since Le
Roy was not a professional printer" (48). Kenneth Povey found
all the variants in Allde's 1624 edition of Massinger's *The
Bonds-man* reconcilable with Moxon's procedure (48).
"It is doubly a pity . . . when writers adapt conditions to suit
their theories and then find themselves obliged to discount the
testimony of such an excellent palmer as Moxon" (49). [D. F.
Foxon's note on proofing in 1639 and 1640 (*Library* 5th ser. 25
[1970]151-154) and McKenzie's own note on proof-sheets of
1594 (*Library* 5th ser. 28[1973]1-13), noted above (50-51), both
support McKenzie's ideas of proofing just stated. Hinman's
"far too many obvious errors of all kinds in far too many Folio
pages" (above) is, of course, only a bibliographer's subjective
opinion. Anyone who has worked in an old-fashioned print

shop—or any professor who has checked proof on his own articles and books—has learned never to be surprised at the number and quality of errors to be found at any stage in the printing process.]

8. *Press Figures* (49-53).

"It is most important to note, first, how many discrepancies there are between the records and the printed figures . . . second, the difficulty of assuming continuity of press-crews for any one figure; third, the irrelevance of the highest figure printed . . . to the actual number of presses in use; fourth, that the occasional failures to figure a form are in fact oversights and do not represent work done at a notationally blank press" (52).

9. *Printing Between 1500 and 1800* (53-60).

Bibliographers sometimes stress the vast difference between conditions in the small Elizabethan shops "restricted in number, presses, edition quantities, and apprentices, and therefore constantly under pressure and operating an essentially uncomplicated, balanced production schedule" (53-54) and conditions in the eighteenth-century houses of (to use Todd's words) "mass production, where not a few but hundreds of pages of type may be retained and repeatedly returned to press, where . . . batteries of pressmen and compositors may produce, in a matter of hours, editions running into thousands of copies, where not one but several books may be put to press concurrently by the same personnel" (59).

But is there "much conclusive evidence" of this difference? There was "expansion of the trade" but with a very few exceptions, the eighteenth century brought only "proliferation, multiple establishments, not an exceptional growth in any one. The fundamental conditions of work in each remain unchanged". As to presses: One might "ask quite directly how Ackers' and the Bowyers' three-, four-, and five-press shops of the 1730s differ from those of Barker, Wolf, Day, Denham, all of whom had more than three presses and the other six printers who in 1583 had three presses each." As to printers limited to two presses in 1615 and 1623, "there is no evidence at all that they conformed . . . and much that they refused to." For that matter, in the eighteenth century "how many had two [presses]; how many had only one? In the second week of October 1732 even Bowyer had only two" (57).

As for edition sizes: "Out of some 514 books printed by Strahan between 1738 and 1785, only 43 were printed in 2000 copies or more, and of these only 15 were in editions of 3000 or more." Much of the lost ephemera of the sixteenth and seventeenth centuries (almanacks, text books, etc.) were required in multiple editions. Of specific major works we have: Psalms in metre (1585) 4000 copies; ABC and Little Catechism (1585) 10,000. In three years during the early 1630s Cambridge printers provided one work in 18,000 copies, one in 12,000, two in 6,000 each, and at least seven in 3000 or more. "But the major evidence of large editions . . . is the complaints from journeymen" about large editions in violation of regulations (58-59).

Although "*some* 18th-century books are the products of conditions of greater complexity . . . the case for any really radical difference between the centuries would seem to have been over-stated. . . . I have tried to suggest that all printing houses were more alike over the years than many bibliographers are prepared to allow . . . most important of all in printing several jobs concurrently" (60).

So much for the Prophet. Study of the printer in the years since McKerrow began mildly enough; it now huffs and it puffs and it may blow the house down.

7. *Enter the Stepchildren*

"Most bibliographers are also university teachers and many of them suffer from schizophrenia. I do not refer to that familiar disease which makes us scholars by day and diaper washers by night, but that split in the man betwen Graduate Seminar number 520 in Bibliography and Freshman Intro. to Fic. 109. How many of us make bibliographical truths part of our daily lives or attempt to inspire our graduate students so to do? In this respect many bibliographers are like socialists and Christians: walking arguments for the weakness of the cause."

Thus wrote Bruce Harkness (65) in "Bibliography and the Novelistic Fallacy" (*SB* 12[1959]59-73). To prove his point he cited, after other examples, Fitzgerald's *The Great Gatsby*. He suggested that the *Three Novels* edition ("the best present text") and the Student's Edition "will be the ones most used in colleges for some time." Yet "in *Three Novels*, we have . . . 1. A book which nowhere gives the . . . authority for seventy-five changes, all . . . posthumously printed. 2. One which fails to make use of all of Fitzgerald's corrections. 3. One which contains thirty-seven changes which Fitzgerald did not authorize. . . . 4. A book which contains at least fifteen quite bad readings, one of which is of the highest structural importance" (73).

The modern novel is only one of Bibliography's stepchildren. For instance, Edwin Wolf 2nd presented convincing "Evidence Indicating the Need for Some Bibliographical Analysis of American-Printed Historical Works" (BSA *Papers* 63[1969]261-277). His examples are from the later eighteenth century, but the need exists in other periods also and for other kinds of publications.

Until quite recently bibliographers have paid little attention to most books printed since about 1800. For this there are, no doubt, many reasons. During the past two centuries the making of a book has become ever more mechanized; to understand it is a complicated business, and the physical book itself is less exciting than its ancestor which owed so much variety to individual hands and minds. Moreover, what is plentiful seems surely not worth too much. Whatever the reason for the neglect, in 1945 Michael Sadleir was able to describe, very briefly indeed but quite adequately, what had been done with nineteenth-century books (*Stud. in Retro.*, 146-158); and in 1959 Matthew J. Bruccoli performed a similar service for twentieth-century books (*Library Trends* 7[1959]566-573). Only in 1949 did we have a full-dress bibliographical treatment of nineteenth- and twentieth-century books with Bowers 353-453; and only in 1972 a full discussion of the machine-press period (1800-1950) in Philip Gaskell's *A New Introduction to Bibliography* (1972)189-310.

For the startling developments in printing since 1950 bibliographers still have no adequate account. James Moran's "Film-setting—Bibliographical Implications" (*Library* 5th ser. 15 [1960]231-245) with its list of "Filmset Incunabula" is a rare bird.

During the past three decades or so, many bibliographers have clustered around the stepchildren in a flurry of solicitous attention. Some of this attention has been bibliographical; some has been something else again.

With Kathleen Tillotson's "*Oliver Twist* in Three Volumes" (*Library* 5th ser. 18[1963]113-132) we are on familiar ground: study of the book as a physical object and study of records of printing and publication. There are title pages with the dates of four consecutive years (113), printing in three months (116), division of copy between printing houses (117), a new title leaf with author's name changed (121), a second edition created by simply inserting the edition words in the form (124), resetting of some gatherings (127), work of different compositors (128-129), a third edition which was simply a reissue with new titles and additional matter (130).

Again we are on familiar ground with William B. Todd's fascinating and spritely "The White House Transcripts" (BSA *Papers* 68[1974]267-296). Here is a book "particularly amenable to such well-established techniques as compositor identification according to orthography or stylistic habits, discrimination of type-forms and patterns, the use of dashes or other devices for expurgated material, the causes of erratic pagination and, particularly for suspect documents, the evidence of irregular and truncated typescripts. The typewriters employed will be critical" (268).

G. Thomas Tanselle's "Millay's *Renascence* and *Second April*: A bibliographical Study" (*Library* 5th ser. 19[1964]175-186) had a thorough bibliographical description of each book followed by evidence leading to the conclusion: "In both cases the type must have been distributed after the first printing . . . and then, when it became necessary . . . a second edition was set up. After that, both books were printed from these new plates at the same times on the same kinds of paper—in September and December 1921, and April and October 1924" (186).

The first editions of *Uncle Tom's Cabin* were the subject of a bibliographical study by E. Bruce Kirkham (BSA *Papers* 65 [1971]365-382) "drawn from 288 copies of the earliest issues, i.e., the first through 120th thousand" (368). It included title transcriptions, collation by gatherings, discussion of bindings. By examination of copies of Edith Wharton's *The Children*, Matthew J. Bruccoli showed that what had passed for the first printing "actually consists of two printings from duplicate plates; furthermore, both these printings include two states" and later there were "more hidden printings" (*SB* 15[1962]269-273). Bruccoli also examined problems created by the use of duplicate plates in modern printing (BSA *Papers* 54[1960]83-88) and by reimpressions from the same plates within a given edition (BSA *Papers* 57[1963]42-49). Oliver L. Steele demonstrated "Half-Sheet Imposition of Eight-leaf Quires in Formes of Thirty-Two and Sixty-Four Pages" in two modern books printed at cylinder presses, Cabell's *Jurgen* (1919) and *Gallantry* (1907) in *SB* 15 (1962)274-278. Jean Muir Rogers and Gordon Stein distinguished printings, states, and editions of Hemingway's *Men Without Women* by such means as weight of the paper, a page number, and two states of a dust jacket (BSA *Papers* 64[1970]210-213). By binding, dust jacket, and cheap paper, Charlotte M. Winzeler proved that the 1910 ghost edition of John Millington Synge's plays was simply a cheap reprint issued later from plates of the 1910 edition of Synge's plays (*Library* 5th ser. 28[1973]158-159).

Some bibliographers dealt with particular aspects of book production. A few examples follow: In the area of the history of publishing, for instance, Anna E. C. Simoni wrote of "Dutch Clandestine Printing, 1940-1945" (*Library* 5th ser. 27[1972]1-22) a story as intriguing as that of English tracts printed on the continent during the Reformation. Giles Barber (*Library* 5th ser. 16[1961]267-286) and James J. Barnes (*Library* 5th ser. 25[1970] 294-313) traced the history of the publishing of English books (many piratical) by Galignani's in France during the first half of the nineteenth century.

"The Forms of Twentieth-Century Cancels" by John Cook Wyllie (BSA *Papers* 47[1953]95-112) discussed a wide variety ranging from cancelled leaves and gatherings to cancelled bindings and dust jackets; G. Thomas Tanselle had a supplement in

BSA *Papers* 68(1974)69-71. Elizabeth A. Swaim told of post-production censorship which caused a gathering in Owen Wister's *Roosevelt* (1930) to be cancelled (*SB* 27[1974]290-293). In this era the publisher's binding became part of the book as a physical object. Michael Sadleir's *The Evolution of Publishers' Binding Styles, 1770-1900* (1930), J. W. Carter's *Binding Variants in English Publishing, 1820-1900* (1932), and Carter's *Publishers' Cloth, 1820-1900* (1938) were followed by a number of articles and books. The dust cover is also part of the physical book—e.g., G. Thomas Tanselle's "Book-Jackets, Blurbs, and Bibliographers" (*Library* 5th ser. 26[1971]91-134).

Serial publication and three-volume publication of novels appeared in a number of studies—e.g., Charles E. Lauterbach and Edward S. Lauterbach, "The Nineteenth Century Three Volume Novel" (BSA *Papers* 51[1957]263-302) and Douglas C. Ewing, "The Three-Volume Novel" (BSA *Papers* 61[1967]201-207). "A novel in nineteen paper-wrappered parts is not the same book as the same words in the same order, printed in a squat, pudgy, little ill-printed paper-covered volume; nor is a book which was written to be published in three octavo volumes the same as one intended for one, two, four or more volumes" (Ewing 205-206).

Perhaps the most famous book in this group was John Carter and Graham Pollard's *An Enquiry into the Nature of Certain Nineteenth Century Pamphlets* (1934) on the forgeries of Thomas J. Wise. It has been followed by a horde of books and articles on Wise and the growing list of his nefarious activities.

Finally we shall look briefly at a few studies in a group which raises a special problem.

By means of corrected proofsheets, Francis Russell Hart was able to "depict the processes of composition and revision through which a degree of reticence developed" (3) in John Lockhart's life of Scott (*SB*14[1961]2-22). Drastic revisions of Scott's letters, touched up conversations, removal of some material thought likely to give offense—with these and other not always disinterested devices urged by Scott's friends and associates, the work moved through the proofsheets toward Victorian respectability.

In "Notes on the Unrevised Galleys of Faulkner's *Sanctuary*" (*SB* 8[1956]195-208) Linton Massey told how Faulkner revised what he called "the most horrific tale I could imagine" at sight of which his publisher "wrote me immediately, 'Good God, I can't publish this. We'd both be in jail. . . . ' " (197). Massey suggested Faulkner's attitude as he rewrote from the offending galleys: "Be heartless, therefore, in stamping this pattern of evil; be unrelenting; be direct. Cut here; rewrite there, transpose, elaborate, condense. In some such fashion, and with a minimum of effort, Faulkner altered the entire focus and meaning of the book" (204).

Others also have written about proof revisions—e.g., Dale Kramer on Hardy's *The Woodlanders* (*SB* 20[1967]135-150) showing that Hardy was a "conscientious craftsman" (150); Robert Henry Miller on Raymond Chandler's *The Long Goodbye* (BSA *Papers* 63[1969]279-290) showing Chandler as a "conscientious writer" who wanted "accurate, polished printed texts of his works" (279); and Robert E. Scholes on James Joyce's *Dubliners* (*SB* 15[1962]191-205) showing, among other things, "the now-familiar pattern of attempted censorship" (193). John Pfordresher's "A Bibliographic History of Alfred Tennyson's *Idylls of the King*" (*SB* 26[1973] 193-218) included a bibliography of manuscripts, printer's proofs, and printed editions, but only those editions "which play a significant part in the evolution of the text" (196-199). The bulk of the study, however, was a complex story ranging over many years of Tennyson's life and accounting for a great variety of manuscripts and trial proofs and revisions—a detailed history of the gradual development of the poem in Tennyson's mind.

"*The Spoils of Poynton*: Revisions and Editions" by S. P. Rosenbaum (*SB* 19[1966]161-174): James "carefully revised each of the first three texts" with "nearly 3,400 changes . . . between the four texts" ranging "from the deletion of a comma to the change of the novel's title" (163). "Many of the changes are inexplicable" (172). James considered the frontispiece an integral part of the work (173-174). Francis E. Skipp showed how Thomas Wolfe's editor at Scribners drastically cut the manuscript for *Of Time and the River* removing much that was excellent and much that was banal (BSA *Papers* 64[1970]313-322). The differing chapter numbers in various editions of Dickens' *Oliver Twist* "may suggest his moving away from the purely picaresque novel of incident to a scene structured form" (343 in Joan Schweitzer, BSA *Papers* 60[1966]337-343). Selwyn H. Goodacre's study of "Lewis Carroll's 1887 Corrections to *Alice*" (*Library* 5th ser. 28[1973]131-146) showed that "obviously there is still a need for a definitive edition" (146).

All such work is interesting; some is fascinating. And yet: proof sheets, censorship, development of an author's style or his attitude toward a particular book, conscientious craftsmanship, definitive editions—what have these to do with the book as a physical object? Are such studies truly bibliography? Or are they literary history, literary criticism, textual criticism? The question haunts many studies of books printed since 1800.

So the stepchildren came into their own—and more.

8. *The Captive Bride*

The bibliographer, we have found, serves (among other people) the textual critic, the scholar who seeks to establish precisely an author's original words and phrases (12). Yet we have also noted that now and then the bibliographer wanders into the textual critic's province—e.g., when he studies compositors (57) and when he studies the changing text of some more modern works (57). On such occasions he moves in some degree from study of the book as a physical object to study of the message which that physical object carries.

For many centuries before they received their modern names— perhaps as long ago as the Alexandrian Library—bibliographer and textual critic worked harmoniously side by side each at his own trade. Then fifty years ago McKerrow wrote with some concern about a shift in this ancient partnership.

McKerrow insisted that he had written "a help-book for literary students. I wish there to be no misunderstanding about this. It is not a hand-book for students of printing or of general bibliography. Still less is it intended for book-collectors. I . . . have kept before me throughout the problem of the relation of the printed book to the written work of the author" (vi). "We are all now for 'bibliographical' methods. . . . But there is much more in these modern methods of research than used to be understood by 'bibliography,' and I am not sure that the recent extensions of the term have been altogether justifiable. The virtue of bibliography . . . was its definiteness . . . that two persons of reasonable intelligence following the same line of bibliographical argument would inevitably arrive at the same conclusion. . . . There is a great group of questions concerning the transmission of texts . . . which, from the large amount of conjecture that must necessarily enter into any solution of them, differ entirely from the purely bibliographical problems to which we have been accustomed in the past. A theory, for example, which should seek to explain evident disturbances . . . in the text . . . by postulating a corrected manuscript in which . . . later additions had been so placed that the point where they should be inserted had been misunderstood by the copyist or printer . . . is certainly in a sense bibliographical. If, however, it involves, as it very often does, . . . the theorist's literary judgement of stylistic difference . . . it is . . . very different . . . from such evidence of insertion . . . as may be derived from a disturbance of the regular practice of the compositor, such as an increase in the number of lines to the page. There will in the future be much to say about these newer kinds of bibliographical investigation, but they belong rather to the sphere of textual criticism than to formal bibliography and I do not propose to touch upon them here" (2-3).

"The numerous processes through which all books pass are perfectly simple. . . . What is needed is that they shall be grasped so clearly as to be constantly present to the mind of the student"; so he sees the book not only as literature, "but also from the points of view of those who composed, corrected, printed, folded, and bound it; in short . . . he sees it not only as a unit but as an assemblage of parts, each of which is the result of a clearly apprehended series of processes. Once he does this he will find that the material book, apart altogether from its literary content, can be a thing of surprising interest" (4).

That was in 1927. In 1945 F. P. Wilson took the same "material book" approach: "To a formal bibliographer a book is not the life-blood of a master spirit but a collection of pieces of paper with printing on them. He pursues his task of extracting from his material the utmost evidence that it will yield, indifferent to the question whether his work will be of use to the editor or the critic" (*Stud. in Retro.* 95). But Wilson announced that the editor of Shakespeare "must now be bibliographer as well as critic" (121). The "new bibliography," he concluded, "has indeed profoundly changed editorial principle and practice" (134).

In the same volume Greg again defined bibliography as "the study of books as material objects," and he insisted that "bibliography has nothing whatever to do with the subject or literary content of the book" (24). He praised McKerrow for understanding so clearly that "a training in bibliography was essential for any student who aspired to do original literary research of a textual nature," for writing such a "notable work," and for his "rather conservative view of the scope of bibliography" which kept him "free from any temptation to stretch its boundaries to embrace any but the most material facts" (29). On the very next page Greg pulled his own stretcher: The "relationship of manuscripts to one another, and the relationship of printed editions to one another are . . . bibliographical facts . . . indeed, the whole question of the transmission of literary texts, through the agency of scribes on the one hand and of the printing press on the other, is in essence bibliographical. Are not the physical vehicles of that transmission the very material books that . . . form the proper study of bibliography? Thus bibliography and textual criticism appear to interlock in a manner that makes it difficult if not impossible to separate their respective fields and leads one to wonder whether it may not in the end be necessary to bring most textual criticism within the province of bibliography" (30).

On this side of the Atlantic, Bowers also was wondering as he wrote "Some Relations of Bibliography to Editorial Problems" (*SB* 3[1950-51]37-62). "I should be less than candid if I tried to pretend that the immediate or even the chief aim of . . . bibliographical scholars was to serve as the sons of Martha to textual criticism" (41). "It is perhaps absurd to set up too sharp

a distinction between textual critics and textual bibliographers"
(42). With the term "textual bibliographers" we learn of another
chamber built onto the many-chambered mansion of Bibliography. But the adjective is soon dropped. "We may put it,
therefore, that bibliography is neither a usurper nor a poor
relation in the field of textual criticism, but rather its founda-
tion, the grammar of the subject" (43). The "grammar" idea
perhaps echoes "W. W. Greg's acute phrase" that Bibliography
"is the grammar of literary investigation" cited by Bowers (37),
a phrase which Greg had himself actually quoted from W. A.
Copinger as Thorpe (90, n. 14) pointed out. In summary: (1)
"textual criticism and analytical bibliography in their purest
states are . . . independent arts"; (2) "textual criticism cannot
controvert accurate bibliography . . . however, the two often
join in attacking certain problems of texts"; (3) "neither method
can achieve definitive textual results . . . without reference to
the other" (60-61). Finally: "One of the chief functions of textual
bibliography is to try to pierce this veil of the printing process
and to restore, however imperfectly, the authority of the manuscript which we know only through its printed . . . form"
(61-62). And so "Bibliography" in the Bowers essay's title really
means bibliography and/or analytical bibliography and/or
accurate bibliography and/or textual bibliography.

"Textual Bibliography" caught on. It appeared even in non-
bibliographical publications. In *Library Trends* (7 [1959]495),
for instance, Harold Lancour's outline of bibliography listed
Textual Bibliography (defined "Study and comparison of texts
and their transmission through editions and printings") as one
of the three divisions of "Analytical or Critical Bibliography";
the other two divisions are Historical Bibliography ("Placing
and dating of individual books"), and Descriptive Bibliography
("Identification of the 'ideal copy' and all its variants"). Beginning in the late fifties the *Encyclopaedia Britannica* article on
"Bibliography" (by Bowers) listed Textual Bibliography as one
of the four branches of Bibliography (the other three are Enumerative (or Systematic), Analytical (or Critical), and Descriptive.
The "grammar" had now become the "backbone of textual
criticism" and it was defined as "the application of analytical
bibliography" to the three major specific problems of the textual

critic: (1) the analysis of the physical characteristics of an extant manuscript; (2) the recovery of the characteristics of a lost manuscript from the details of the print; and (3) the study of the transmission of the text.

Bowers later came back with a book: *Bibliography and Textual Criticism* (1964). The bibliographer, he confessed (5), does much which often has little "immediate and practical bearing on the solution of specific textual difficulties"; instead, the bibliographer asks other questions: How many presses printed the book? How many skeleton forms and what was the sequence of their use? Did the compositor set the pages in normal sequence or did he set by forms after casting off copy? How many compositors were there and how can we tell the work of each? How did the various editions relate to each other? Even worse, the answers are often provisional; and bibliographers differ among themselves as to which answers are correct.

So Bowers wanted to explain "the application of analytical bibliography to the main problems of textual criticism" (7) with special reference to Elizabethan drama. Sections on analytical and textual bibliography and the interpretation of various kinds of evidence were lavishly adorned with examples drawn from his long experience as distinguished teacher and practicing bibliographer. He closed with a detailed concrete illustration of the sort of thing he had in mind: a compositor study applied to the problem of determining the copy-text of the Folio *Othello*.

With regard to textual bibliography: "The relation of analytical to textual bibliography, and thence—immediately—to textual criticism, *is* subject to misinterpretation, principally because analytical bibliography thereby invades a field that has customarily been pre-empted by some form of literary criticism" (26). Thus, bibliography is indeed an invader, but it invades only an area whose present occupant had itself "pre-empted" the field. In textual bibliography "the contents—the author's words—are not treated primarily as symbols instantaneously to be resolved into meaningful concepts in the mind. Instead, at least at the start, the words and punctuation are thought of primarily as simple inked shapes, imprinted on paper from pieces of metal systematically selected and arranged by . . . the compositor. This point of view leads to another . . . concept of the book as a

tangible object, in which internal and external form impercep-
tibly merge into one. Accordingly, the function of textual bibliography is to treat these imprinted shapes . . . without primary
concern for their symbolic value as conceptual organism . . .
but, instead, as impersonal and non-conceptual inked prints.
. . . To determine the exact details of the mechanical process
that produced the sequence of these inked shapes . . . is the
chief end of textual bibliography. . . . The heart of the method
consists in supplying a mechanical explanation for all mechanically produced phenomena whenever such an explanation can
be arrived at on the recoverable evidence." On the other hand,
a "critical explanation" gives "reasons for the phenomena that
are historical or literary and thus ultimately refer to values, or
opinion, as the basis for judgement" (27-28). All this is reminiscent of Greg's position (see above 93).

The argument for such a point of view hinges on the examples;
we shall look briefly at a few.

Page 34: Proof that two half sheets were printed in one form
means to Bowers that "one agent must have marked the pages for
correction in both half sheets" at the same time. This conclusion
is, indeed, as Bowers says, "non-literary and impersonal," but
is it necessarily correct? It may be at least possible that one or
more alterations could have been made during the *process* of
printing and not just at the one time the "one agent" indicated
corrections. Certainly on page 39 such a possibility is admitted
for another book.

Page 45, footnote 1: "Unless we are to assume that the proof-
reader referred to copy and misread what he saw there (and we
have no evidence that he did so refer in correcting this
forme). . . ." John Jones may stay out of jail because of lack of
evidence, but lack of evidence to the contrary does not *prove*
that John is an honest man.

Page 157, Note B: "If Q is a memorially reconstructed 'bad
quarto', as seems likely, its reading derives ultimately from the
prompt-book. If the copy for the Folio also derives ultimately
from the prompt-book, as I believe, then F and Q could both
print the same error if the source of the error were the prompt-
book. Thus Sisson's argument collapses." Or *would* collapse if

the Bowers "ifs" were proved facts instead of "ifs". Bowers concludes the Note with another "if," another "as I believe," and an appeal to "the simple evidence of the sense." What ever happened to study of the book as a material object?

Page 51: "It is a physical fact that the place in which the action of Dekker and Massinger's *Virgin Martyr* is laid is spelled *Cesarea* in some scenes and in others *Caesarea*, and that the two spellings are never mixed in one scene. That this spelling difference, combined with other spelling and punctuation differences, distinguishes scenes written by the two authors is not a physical fact . . . but instead is a hypothesis. If the hypothesis comes to be generally accepted after considerable testing, the authorship of the different scenes may be accepted as factually demonstrated." Is then, "generally accepted" (even after "considerable testing") the same as "factually demonstrated"? On page 13 Bowers had written of the same play: "enough consistent spelling variation is present in the printed text, set by a single compositor, to provide quite enough evidence for assigning the authorship of every scene to one or other playwright." For two other collaborated plays, each with word difference sections like those in the *Virgin Martyr*, Bowers had suggested that the different sections ofthe manuscript could have been the work of different scribes as easily as the work of different authors (*Lust's Dominion*—Cardinal/Mendoza [9-11] and *I Henry VI*—Burgundy/Burgonie [30, Note A]). "Whether the bibliographically ascertained difference in the manuscript reflects a change of authorship, or not, is thereupon almost exclusively the decision of the literary critic working with questions of style and content" (11).

Page 57: "Occurrences in which bibliographical analysis can supply the whole answer to textual cruxes are fairly limited. For every example like *shortly* versus *thereby* in Hamlet, or *sullied* versus *solid* flesh, where an immediate bibliographical basis for decision can exist, there are hundreds that can rely only on the general guidance of bibliographical findings that have established the derivation and relationship of the texts as a whole." We shall look at these two cases of "immediate bibliographical basis":

Shortly/thereby (Bowers 44-45). Three copies of the Second Quarto of *Hamlet* read at v.i.321, "An houre of quiet *thirtie* shall we see"; the other three preserved copies read *thereby* instead of *thirtie*. The Shakespeare Folio reads, "An houre of quiet *shortly* shall we see." The first reading is in the "uncorrected state of the outer forme of sheet N" as "originally set by the compositor. It is bibliographically clear that *thereby* is the proof-reader's alteration, and critically that it is his rationalization of *thirtie*, without reference to copy. . . . Once we learn that *thirtie* was what the compositor set, we may discuss with the palaeographer whether the Folio variant *shortly* might have been misread in the Q2 manuscript as *thirtie*; and on the affirmative the critic may adopt the Folio reading with some confidence" because "we must assume" it was in "the manuscript used in the preparation of the Folio text" and because it was "very likely . . . in the manuscript behind Q2." In this analysis, it is the textual critic who decides (without evidence) that the proof-reader changed *thirtie* to *thereby* "without reference to copy," and it is the textual critic who decides (without evidence except that the error is palaeographically possible) that the compositor set the manuscript *shortly* as *thirtie* even though the line then made no sense.

Sullied/solid. Bowers does not again refer to these variants in his book. Thorpe (97): "Some bibliographers seem to approach verbal assault on one another, even in connection with a reading (like Hamlet's 'solid' or 'sullied' flesh) about which it is alleged that there is physical evidence, not subject to opinion, to reach an indisputable conclusion—though every conclusion reached by one bibliographer is disputed by another"; and in footnote 33 Thorpe cites a few of the "numerous bibliographical disquisitions on this crux" (*solid/sullied*), among them one by Bowers.

Are *shortly/thereby* and *sullied/solid* truly examples of "immediate bibliographical basis"?

Page 206: Under the index entry "variants" forty-five sets of variant readings are listed. Reference to the pages where these readings are discussed reinforces Bowers' statement, "Occurrences in which bibliographical analysis can supply the whole answer to textual cruxes are fairly limited" (57). Of these forty-five sets of readings, very few are solved—or even helped to solution—by bibliographical analysis. ("Very few" is not a precise figure because different readers will have different opinions as to which sets should be included.)

Pages 152-154: In the Shakespeare Folio *Richard III*, lines 533-536 appear as follows:

> *Cat.* My liege, the Duke of Buckingham is taken,
> That is the best newes: that the Earle of Richmond
> Is with a mighty power Landed at Milford,
> Is colder Newes, but yet they must be told.

In Q1 and in Q3 line 536 reads:

> Is colder tidings, yet they must be told.

In Q5 and in Q6 the line reads:

> Is colder Newes, yet they must be told.

It is the "natural assumption" that "F merely followed Q6" (154) with, of course, the "metrically required but sophisticated addition *but*" (153). On the other hand, one might "conjecture that line 534 *That is the best newes* independently contaminated the Folio compositor's memory in line 536 (while setting from Q3) as it manifestly had the Q5 compositor's" (153). But "line 534 containing *That is the best newes* . . . is the last line of Folio sig. s6r, a page set completely by Compositor A. Line 535 begins sig. s6v, a page set wholly by Compositor B . . . B would have started to set where his copy was marked, with the first line beginning *Is with a mighty power*, and would have had no occasion to read the preceding line that had been already set by A" (153-154). This psychoanalysis of B in his absence makes him a dull, mechanical, careless man who could begin setting type in the middle of a train of thought with no curiosity about what had gone before and no wish to be sure that he was carrying on exactly as the preceding words demanded. Perhaps he was.

So much for examples of textual bibliography at work. It seems possible that some readers of Bowers may now and then believe that an example does not rely on "a mechanical explanation for all mechanically produced phenomena," that it instead suggests "reasons for the phenomena that are historical or literary and thus ultimately refer to values, or opinion, as the basis for judgement" (see above 95-96).

One of the most recent statements on "textual bibliography" is Gaskell's chapter (336-360). It opens: "Traditionally the function of textual criticism has been to follow the threads of transmission back from an existing document and to try to restore its text as closely as possible to the form it originally took in the author's manuscript." He then cites work on the Bible and classical and medieval authors. "Textual bibliography is textual criticism adapted to the analogous but not identical problems of editing printed texts" (336). So the *New Introduction to Bibliography,* unlike the first *Introduction* (see 92 above), marched firmly into the realm of textual criticism.

A few scholars have, like McKerrow, protested undue expansion of bibliography—e.g., Geoffrey Keynes (*Library* 5th ser. 8[1953]66) suggested that "The tendency to exaggerate the claims of bibliography . . . is perhaps to be recognized as a psychological frustration." Alice Walker remarked that "it is, I suppose, generally agreed that the bibliographer is best qualified to construct a stemma for printed books; but, unless the recension provides an editor with a fool-proof text, it is the business of the textual critic to discriminate between true and false readings. Let us, therefore, use the traditional term 'textual criticism,' so that everyone knows what we are talking about" (*Library* 5th ser. 16[1961]311). E. A. J. Honigman complained: "Of late the tendency has been to identify textual criticism with 'scientific bibliography.' Fredson Bowers, despite the acknowledged importance of his work, sometimes adds to the confusion by standing beside a textual crux and going through scientific bibliographical motions. The bibliographical part of the argument consists of 'mechanical evidence,' rigorous method, and irresistible logic, and yet its relevance to a specific crux may involve an awkward jump" (*Library* 5th ser. 23[1968]264).

Roy Stokes was more gentle but equally firm: "No one would

attempt to make bibliography play a larger part in textual problems than the very nature of the evidence makes practicable. No one would attempt to justify a claim that bibliography comprises the whole of textual criticism. The recognition which bibliographers now seek should be that textual criticism rests on a firm basis of historical, literary, philological, and bibliographical evidence. The first three have long been accepted as valid evidence, the fourth can now be regarded as of equal repute even if not invariably of equal importance" (155-56).

With an ironic smile Thorpe greeted "those who would make textual criticism a branch of bibliography. This is a game that two can play. One can readily imagine the other party serving: the ambitious textual critic describes the four forms of textual criticism, with the fourth as 'bibliographic textual criticism' —which is made to encompass all textual evidence that derives from an examination of the production of books and manuscripts as physical objects—and with bibliography as one branch of textual criticism. I might, under those circumstances, find myself writing about the way in which textual criticism was distorting bibliography" (101).

Elsewhere Thorpe complained: "My experience as a textual editor has been that there is usually no bibliographical evidence to use in trying to solve the most troublesome problems that I have encountered. . . . Moreover, there is a good deal of argument among bibliographers as to what constitutes a bibliographical 'fact' " (96-97); we have noticed this problem before. Much in Thorpe's book, particularly in the chapters on "The Province of Textual Criticism" and "Textual Analysis," might readily appear (with only a few slight changes) in a bibliographer's book in a chapter called "Textual Bibliography." It may be unlikely, however, that the bibliographer's book would contain Thorpe's suggestion "that the issues which I have been outlining simply prove to superior beings that fleas have other fleas to bite them or that a new Dunciad would be the only suitable method for putting us all in our places" (101).

Thorpe felt, however, that the "bibliographically oriented editor tends to report very fully on every irregularity, even when it causes no disturbance in the text" (102); and he was particularly critical of the "strongly bibliographical cast" (103) of the *Statement of Editorial Principles* by the Modern Language Association's Center for Editions of American Authors (69-79 and 103-104). This elaborate project has, indeed, been the subject of much controversy ranging from savage attacks such as Edmund Wilson's *The Fruits of the MLA* (1968) to amused histories such as Benjamin DeMott's account of "The Battle of the Books" (*New York Times Book Review* [Oct. 17, 1971]58-60).

So the captive bride had a new name thrust upon her. But hers is an old, old story called "By Any Other Name."

9. *It Is Not True: Anatomy of a Litany*

"McKerrow Revisited" by Fredson Bowers (BSA *Papers* 67 [1973]109-124) is a review article of Philip Gaskell's *A New Introduction to Bibliography* (1972). Halfway through it is a litany of fifteen statements each beginning "It is not true" (118-119). These statements are quoted or summarized below, each accompanied by Gaskell's remark which provoked it and by a comment:

1. *Bowers*: "It is not true, except in folio works, that setting by formes was a 'common' practice in English printing up to the mid-seventeenth century."

Gaskell (41): "Setting by formes appears to have been a common practice in English and in some continental printing up to the mid seventeenth century". As evidence he cites the Bond article described above (45) and "study of recurring types" in "London-printed verse plays of the later sixteenth and early seventeenth century" (apparently such as that considered above, 48-50).

Comment: The Bowers remark is undocumented; in another connection (116, n. 4) he had noted the McKenzie article on setting by forms in quarto in 1594 (see above 50-51). On the other hand, Gaskell cites only the Bond study (seven books by three printers) and unspecified "study of recurring types." Are these examples, even with the addition of the McKenzie study, enough to prove that setting by forms was "common practice"?

2. *Bowers*: "It is not true that a 'high proportion' of plays of the later sixteenth and early seventeenth centuries were set by formes, folios again excepted".

Gaskell (42): The "study of recurring types" in such plays (see above) "proves that a high proportion of them were set by formes, individual pieces of type being found in both formes of a pair; the first folio of Shakespeare (London 1623) is only the most celebrated example" (with reference to Hinman's book).

Comment: As with No. 1, we have Bowers undocumented, Gaskell vaguely documented. How prove or disprove "high proportion"?

3. *Bowers*: "It is not true that setting by formes in books other than quired folios saved enough type to make it worthwhile."

Gaskell (42): "The reason for setting by formes is not entirely obvious." It "certainly makes a limited stock of type go further, and some . . . who set by formes around 1600 were chronically short of type. But other printers who were not short of type also set by formes, Plantin, for instance . . . up to about 1565. . . . The method of 'half-sheet imposition' . . . saves just as much type as setting by formes in foldings other than folio, and is much easier to manage . . . Moxon mentioned [setting by forms] in 1683 only to dismiss it as undesirable."

Comment: The Bowers statement is undocumented; the Gaskell statement may be misleading. How much type saved would be "worthwhile" (Bowers)? Why is the reason for setting by forms "not entirely obvious" (Gaskell)? Perhaps Moxon (210-211), quoted in full above (43), suggests some answers. Moxon did not, as Gaskell has it, mention setting by forms "only to dismiss it." Moxon said that in setting type for a folio gathering of more than two leaves, the "wise compositor" will immobilize type in pages already set but not yet imposed only to the extent that he "have a fount of letter large enough"; sometimes the supply of type is "large enough" only if he will cast off copy and set by forms. Such a principle would apply to all books. The

Bowers "worthwhile" would vary from book to book and day to day and shop to shop. A folio with 6-leaf gatherings, a quarto with 8-leaf gatherings, two books being set in the same shop in the same type in the same time, a shop with a small supply of the type needed for one book—any of these and similar conditions might make it worthwhile. (Apart from type, the time required for casting off should be figured in.) Perhaps one or more of these considerations answers the Gaskell quest for an "entirely obvious" reason. Half sheet imposition would, indeed, save type; but it would produce only half sheet gatherings and the problem answered by setting by forms is: How produce gatherings each a sheet or more in length if the type is short (for any reason)?

4. *Bowers*: "It is not true that simultaneous shared setting was 'not uncommon' in London about 1600 between different printing houses; nor is it sporting to give . . . as the single evidence . . . the example of King James's coronation souvenir pamphlet, required in huge quantities . . . beyond the capacities of a single shop to produce within the necessary time." Such shared printing was employed for big books such as the Beaumont and Fletcher folio (1647), and it was "fairly common in Restoration play quartos produced in a hurry to take advantage of the author's night" but it "was not common about 1600 except for massive books."

Gaskell (43): "Simultaneous shared setting (especially if it took place in two or more different printing houses, as was not uncommon in London around 1600) might result in pages or sections of irregular length." (Footnote to the parenthetical phrase: "Greg noted several examples in *A Bibliography of the English Printed Drama to the Restoration*, e.g. no. 202.")

Comment: How much is "not uncommon" (Gaskell) or "fairly common" (Bowers)? The Bowers statement is not documented; Gaskell is only somewhat better. The evidence for Gaskell, however, is "not uncommon"; see above (75).

5. *Bowers*: "It is not true that the regular practice of the Elizabethan compositor was to impose the second forme of a sheet immediately after the first, without delay. This easy

generalization ignores a compositor's time schedule as well as the differences between one- and two-skeleton printing."

Gaskell (80): Once imposed, the first form "was virtually a solid slab of wood and metal and, although it did not have a bottom like a tray, it could be moved about or lifted without the type falling out. The compositor therefore pushed it to one side (or stood it on its edge on the floor, leaning against his frame) and proceeded to impose the second forme of the sheet in the same way."

Comment: Neither statement is documented; Bowers' logic is sound. It may be worth noting that if Gaskell's compositor followed Moxon he imposed on a correcting stone "large enough to hold two chases and more" (Moxon 35); generally there would be no need to stand a completed form "on its edge on the floor, leaning against his frame."

6. *Bowers*: "It is not true that it is seldom possible to tell whether half-sheets in quarto or octavo can be determined as printed by single or by twin half-sheet imposition. One of the most elementary of running-title investigations demonstrates by the pattern which method would be employed."

Gaskell (83, 106): "It is seldom possible to tell which method has been used in printing particular half sheets in quarto or octavo." (In a footnote he refers to K. Povey's "On the Diagnosis of Half-Sheet Imposition" (*Library* 5th ser. 11[1956]268-272).)

Comment: How often is "seldom"? Bowers is, of course, correct about running titles; but Gaskell is writing of the period 1500-1800 and readily identifiable individual running titles are not so easily found in the latter half of this period. Povey lists other means of identification such as fore-edges, point-holes, watermarks, and press-figures, but these again are sometimes not helpful. Povey concludes that investigation of half-sheet impositions "should begin with a comparison of" two uncut copies. "The printing procedure must have been one which could give rise to all the points in which the two copies agree and to all those in which they differ" (272).

7. *Bowers*: "It is not true that mistakes in signatures and in

catchwords show that direction-lines were sometimes transferred with the skeleton."

Gaskell (109): "It appears from mistakes in signatures (and
occasionally in catchwords) that direction lines were sometimes
transferred with the skeleton."

Comment: Neither statement is documented. If the compositor
followed Moxon (210), he set the catchword and (when proper)
the signature at the bottom of each page. A direction line "transferred with the skeleton" would interfere with this. But it is my
impression that I have now and then come across signatures and
catchwords such as Gaskell describes.

8. *Bowers*: "It is not true that single-skeleton printing was or
could have been caused by type shortage."

Gaskell (110): "The reason for single skeleton working may
have been shortage of type, not because the skeleton itself was
especially costly or uneconomical of type, but because the printer
could not keep more than a few pages standing at a time and thus
had no need of more than one skeleton; or it may have been some
casual shortage of any of the constituent parts of the skeleton."

Comment: Neither statement is documented. Shortage of type
could, of course, cause casting off and printing by forms; this
would require only one skeleton at a time. If only one press were
available for the job, one skeleton would be enough even if the
type for both forms had been set.

9. *Bowers*: "It is not true that in Elizabethan printing whole-
sheet cancels are ever difficult to identify, since the variant
running-titles or their pattern would be a dead giveaway."

Gaskell (134): "Whole sheets . . . cancelled . . . are usually
difficult to identify unless an uncancelled copy of the sheet
happens to survive. Differences in the paper . . . may give a
clue." In Baskerville's Virgil of 1757 "whole-sheet cancels on
laid paper show up in the wove part of the book." Finally,
"there was generally considerable regularity in the use of
skeleton formes through a hand-printed book, and whole-sheet
cancellation was very likely to interrupt the pattern, often to the
extent of introducing a special set of headlines."

Comment: Here again Gaskell is writing of 1500-1800 and must consider other evidence as well as headlines. Perhaps the Gaskell "usually" applies to the whole period. Perhaps "very likely to interrupt" is more accurate than "dead giveaway."

10. *Bowers*: "It is not true in the Elizabethan period that each edition was distributed by its publisher-wholesaler through numerous retail booksellers."

Gaskell (146): "Each edition was distributed by its publisher-wholesaler (who might also have been its printer) through numerous retail booksellers, each of whom sold a few copies of it over his counter; it was generally the case that printers and publishers themselves also acted as retailers."

Comment: Neither statement is documented.

11. *Bowers*: "It is not true before the Commonwealth that a master could afford to own more presses than he would normally need. The number of presses was rigidly controlled by inspection, and the practice of the Cambridge University Press in 1700 has no bearing."

Gaskell (163-164): "There was no economic need to be short of presses (although on occasion the number of presses was limited by official decree.)" A press cost about one-tenth as much as the type to keep it busy or one-third to one-half the annual earnings of a journeyman. So "the master could afford to own more presses than he would normally need." This meant that the master could add men or lay them off as the flow of business demanded.

Comment: Apparently Gaskell's "afford" is simply economic and he offers as reference his Ph. D. thesis and L. Voet, *The Golden Compasses*, ii. As to the Bowers "afford": there seems to be some evidence that even in the Elizabethan period the number of privately owned presses was not always "rigidly controlled" (McKenzie 54-55). P. W. M. Blayney suggests, however, that McKenzie may be "going too far the other way" (BSA *Papers* 67[1973]441).

12. *Bowers*: "It is not true, despite the evidence of the peculiar Cambridge University Press a hundred years later, that in Eliza-bethan commercial printing shops as many as ten or twelve books

would be printing concurrently in a two-press shop. (This is a fantastic assertion.)"

Gaskell (164): "Books varied so much in size that a balance between composition and press-work could not have been kept if they had been printed serially. . . . Printers therefore had several books in production at once—as many as ten or twelve at a time even in a two-press shop—so that when a man came to the end of a stage in the work, he would be in a position to take up something else, for there was generally something ready to be done." This meant slower work on individual books but more efficient use of plant and men.

Comment: The Bowers statement is not documented. Gaskell refers us to McKenzie. Some of McKenzie's position rests more on logic than on specific facts—e.g. "The documentation that exists for a shop of comparable size in 1700, printing books in editions no larger than those permitted in 1587, makes it clear that productive conditions of enormous complexity involving as many as ten or a dozen jobs at any one time were normal in a small two-press house" (54). Perhaps Gaskell's "ten or twelve at a time" reflects McKenzie's "ten or a dozen jobs at any one time." Perhaps Gaskell's "balance between composition and press-work" achieved by concurrent printing reflects McKenzie's suggestion that "composition and presswork *as a whole* were fairly economically balanced" with concurrent printing (22; see also above 65-66, 68, and 73-74).

13. *Bowers*: "It is not true for the small Elizabethan shop that a book was not necessarily set by a particular compositor or printed at a particular press. The whole 'Pattern of Production' section, pages 160-70, has little or no relation to Elizabethan conditions."

Gaskell (165): "It follows that a book was not necessarily set by a particular compositor or printed at a particular press." A compositor who began a book would not move to another "merely for the sake of change": and "specialist texts such as foreign languages in exotic type might require specialist compositors but experienced men . . . could if necessary take up ordinary work at any point." Thus most books were set by several compositors and even if "one compositor might set a whole book, he would not normally be working on that book alone but would intersperse work on other jobs when it was called for."

Comment: The Bowers statement is undocumented as is also the sweeping indictment of the "Patterns [not Pattern] of Production" section. As in No. 12, Gaskell's remarks are based on McKenzie's logical extension of documented eighteenth-century practice back to earlier days. Any effort to identify the work of individual compositors in a book suggests belief that more than one compositor may have worked on that book.

14. *Bowers*: "It is not true that the markings in the manuscript of *The House of the Seven Gables* suggest that the compositors [*sic*] of each take continued setting up to the end of the current paragraph and would then hand over the extra lines of type to the man who was setting the next take."

Gaskell (194): "The marking of the manuscript suggests that each compositor, on reaching the end of the last type-page of his take, would continue setting up to the end of the current paragraph and would hand over the extra lines of type to the man who was setting the next take (who would have begun at the beginning of the first new paragraph in his copy)."

Comment: The authority cited for each statement is Bowers. Gaskell cites "Old Wine in New Bottles" (J. M. Robson, ed., *Editing Nineteenth-Century Texts* (1967)15-16. Bowers calls the Gaskell statement a "disturbing error in misreporting . . . a secondary source, 'New Wine from Old Bottles' " and suggests it would have been "better scholarship" to have gone to "the primary source, the textual introductions and appendices of the Centenary Edition" of *The House*.

15. *Bowers*: "It is not true that the addition of advertisements should necessarily alter the 'state' of a book: these bound-in added advertisements have no connection with the printing, are arbitrarily added in the bindery, and are untrustworthy guides to priority."

Gaskell (316): One of the "five major classes of variant state" are "Alterations made after some copies have been sold (not involving a new title-page) such as the insertion or cancellation of preliminaries or text pages, or the addition of errata leaves, advertisements, etc."

Comment: The definition is Gaskell's. It may be "customary" or "not customary", but can it be "true" or "false"?

So much for the Litany: It is not true . . . "What is Truth?" said jesting Bibliographer, and would not stay for an answer.

Epilogue

The Cabin

in the Clearing

So much for the Great Leap. Where did it land us?

"Bright lights will cast deep shadows, and I must confess to a feeling of mild despondency about the prospects for analytical bibliography: limited demonstrations there may certainly be, although they may require a lifetime's devotion to make them. . . . Bibliography will simply have to prove itself adequate to conditions of far greater complexity than it has hitherto entertained. . . . But finally, if our basic premise is that bibliography should serve literature or the criticism of literature, it may be thought to do this best, not by disappearing into its own minutiae, but by pursuing the study of printing history to the point where analysis can usefully begin, or by returning—and this is the paradox—to the more directly useful, if less sophisticated, activity of enumerative 'bibliography' "(McKenzie 60-61). Why did McKenzie offer Enumerative Bibliography only as a sort of last forlorn counsel of despair? After all, some seventy years ago one of the most Revered Fathers, A. W. Pollard, also had pronounced it good. "What then is the business of the bibliographer? Primarily and essentially, I should say, the enumeration of books. His is the lowly task of finding out what books exist, and thereby helping to secure their preservation, and furnishing the specialist with information as to the extent of the subject-matter with which he has to deal. . . . When the bibliographer has brought books to light and printed lists of them, whether chronologically, if that be his 'crank,' or under their authors, I submit that he has done a great part of what can reasonably be expected of him" (Quoted by Stokes, 39-40).

Three years later Pollard and Greg wrote "Some Points in Bibliographical Descriptions" (*Trans. Bibl. Soc.* 9[1906-8]31-52, reprinted as A. A. L. Reprint No. 3, 1950). They listed some of the problems and choices, and in an appendix Pollard suggested that in choosing the form of description, bibliographers must consider two factors: "our own object and the nature of the book itself." The object may be (1) "merely to note the existence of the book" or its location; (2) "to indicate its literary contents"; or (3) to describe the book so fully that the "description may be used to ascertain whether other copies are complete and perfect, and whether they belong to exactly the same edition or issue." The "nature of the book" involves the "greater or less amount of information" about the book "given in the book itself"; and "the compactness with which this information is given." After examining several examples "we seem to get four grades: I. Shortest possible form. . . . II. Medium form. . . . IIIA. Standard form for books with complete title-page. IIIB. Standard form for books without title-page, or with a title-page that requires supplementing from the body of the book." Obviously, "the enumeration of books" did not mean simply and always brief listing. Indeed, "our own object and the nature of the book itself" left much to individual judgment.

In a "Memorandum" following Pollard and Greg (*Trans. Bibl. Soc.* 9[1906-8]53-65) Falconer Madan suggested what he called "Degressive Bibliography," long afterward described with comment by John Carter: "It is 'the principle of varying a description according to the difference of the period treated or of the importance of the work to be described.' Newtonian in its simplicity, Einsteinian in its weight, it has yet to penetrate the consciousness of our more pachydermatous bibliographers" (*ABC for Book Collectors*). Degressive Bibliography is often taken to mean briefer and simpler entries in bibliographies. But

Madan, like Pollard and Greg, had four grades of description:
(1.) "full description"—e.g., for incunabula or books from a
special press; (2.) "description"—e.g., for seventeenth-century
books; (3.) "short description"—e.g., for "modern literature";
and (4.) "minimum description"—e.g., "for a mere list of works."
Obviously, "period" and "importance" are both elastic and subjective; they do not of themselves require brief and simple entries
or the opposite, nor does it seem likely that they would guide
today's bibliographer to the same four grades of description with
the same examples. Finally, what bibliographer will ever admit
that his bibliography is not appropriate to the period and importance of the books he lists?

Then came McKerrow: "Firstly, let it be said that there is no
such thing as a standard bibliographical description applicable
to all cases, for the best form to use depends on. . . . 1. The purpose of the description. Are we describing the book as an example
of the art of printing or as the material form of a piece of literature? . . . 2. The date of the book. An incunable . . . requires to be described in quite a different way from a book
printed in the seventeenth century, and that again from a modern work" (145). The application of the criteria, "purpose" and
"date," may, of course, be quite subjective.

In spite of its title, Bowers' *Principles of Bibliographical
Description* (1949) was more concerned with detail of description and standardization of detail than with principles: "The
methods of descriptive bibliography seem to have evolved from
a triple purpose: (1) to furnish a detailed, analytical record of
the physical characteristics of a book which would" identify
and "bring an absent book before a reader's eyes; (2) to provide
an analytical investigation and an ordered arrangement of these
physical facts" to help in textual criticism; and (3) "to approach
both literary and printing or publishing history through the
investigation and recording of appropriate details in a related
series of books" (vii). Bowers sought "to present an organized
bibliographical system . . . based on what I consider to be the
best current practice in scholarly works" (ix).

In much of this Bowers seemed to profess to be setting down
only what was already being done; on one point, however, he
had a quite definite, original opinion: "This highest form of

bibliography should offer a definitive account of a book"
(5, note). Indeed, bibliographical catalogs "differ from a true
bibliography in that they do not pretend to offer the last word
on any book described" (4). Finally, as we have noted before,
Bowers felt that the classification of the various editions, issues,
and states of a book should reflect the history of the printing
of that book. It seems rather unlikely that the "last word" in
the "definitive account" of any book and the history of its
printing can be written unless the bibliographer has examined
all possible variants. But, if he has examined all possible variants, then, surely, description can be cut to a brief statement of
the significant features of each variant.

More recently Thomas Tanselle has pled for "Tolerances in
Bibliographical Description" (*Library* 5th ser. 23[1968]1-12).
"Since the possibilities—both in degree of accuracy and quantity of detail—are infinite, no description of any physical object can ever be complete. It follows that any description,
whether performed by a physicist or a bibliographer, represents
a *limited* accuracy and a *selection* of detail. . . . All that can be
said, then, is that the limits of any description must be determined by the purposes for which it is intended, allowing for the
fact that such limits may vary in individual cases and the future
research may render present standards obsolete" (2-3). Tanselle's
"purposes" is reminiscent of Pollard's "our own object and the
nature of the book itself" and Madan's "period" and "importance."

In "Bibliography Revisited" (*Library* 5th ser. 24[1969]89-128)
Bowers warned against "degressive handlist standards of accuracy" (117); but under controlled conditions, he could "see
nothing wrong with degressive bibliography as applied to a
reduction in the detail awarded a description of the same features
in each edition as in the original full description." He warned
that this reduced detail "must not affect the original research";
otherwise, "we are in danger of moving away from descriptive
bibliography toward enumerative" and if the bibliographer
"decreases his standards of wide and minute comparison of
copies . . . he is no descriptive bibliographer" (126). But
Madan's degressive bibliography dealt only with details of
description, not with reduced standards of accuracy, research
and comparison of copies.

For instance, the checklist of twenty eighteenth-century titles which concluded William B. Todd's "Recurrent Printing" (*SB* 12[1959]189-198) is backed by enough accuracy, research, and comparison of copies to reduce 158 editions (so described by the printer) to only 28. It is true that Todd described the number of copies he examined as "quite inadequate for bibliographical purposes" (192); and, no doubt, further search for copies might turn up more variants. But precisely how many more copies to be "adequate for bibliographical purposes"? Is not the reduction of 158 editions to 28 a respectable "bibliographical purpose"? No matter where we draw the line, the result will always be, as Tanselle says, "*limited* accuracy and a *selection* of detail."

Foxon, indeed, had doubts about the Bowers "ideal of 'definitiveness of research' in the sense that a bibliography can be produced that will not need widespread revision." This was only the first of Foxon's concerns about detailed description. The others follow: (2) "How much use is made in practice of all the detail"? The theory is that the careful reader will discover new variants, but "such variants as are discovered very seldom appear in print." (3) Details do not help the student of printing; "the only way of studying typographical style is to look at the books." (4) By its jargon "bibliography has cut itself off not only from educated men but also from many scholars . . . in a period when bibliographical studies have been most exciting." (5) "The lack of a short-title catalogue for the eighteenth century is now in everyone's mind" (21-24).

And so we come back to McKenzie's Enumerative Bibliography and the cataloger whose practice it is. Whatever else he may or may not be, the cataloger is the pioneer, the builder of the cabin in the clearing. He or his successor may plug a hole in the wall or lay a ghost, add a bathroom or a coat of paint, install a carpet or a chest of drawers. His work may be as simple as Greg I and end as elaborate as Greg II; he may begin with STC I and someone else may come up with STC II. His Census of incunabula in America may yield to Census II and Census II may yield to Census III. For a small library he may give us a one-line entry catalog or he may give us a sophisticated Pforzheimer catalog. At the national level he may give us a Shaw-Shoemaker list or a national union catalog each entry taken chiefly from other catalogers' entries—or he may give us a catalog of the

Library of Congress or of the British Museum each entry taken directly from the books. With Cataloging in Publication he even presents us with books already cataloged. Whatever his cabin may be, it is not the end but the beginning, the point from which we step more confidently into the wilderness beyond.

True, we may not call the cataloger's work analytical bibliography or descriptive bibliography. But is there such a beast as "analytical bibliography" or "descriptive bibliography" or "enumerative bibliography"? We might as well speak of "true truth" or "dark black". All bibliography is analytical; all bibliography is descriptive. It differs from time to time and from job to job only in *detail* of analysis, *detail* of description. Every bibliography is enumerative. All bibliographers are human: some are careful scholars, some are careless drudges, some are so-so.

Where did the Great Leap land us? Probably in better textual criticism, probably in better understanding of printing and publishing. Certainly in better cataloging. Skeleton forms, cast-off copy, compositor, press figures, paper, printing, modern books, textual bibliography—in greater or less degree study of each helps the cataloger more easily and more accurately separate one edition, one issue, one state from another. Whether he himself makes the study or simply reads of the work of someone else the result is the same: a better catalog. And that catalog helps the student of history, life, thought—even the student of bibliography—find the book he needs.

Cat or tiger? Who cares?

Index